THE SKIERS

Also by Jill Bialosky

POETRY
Intruder
Subterranean
The End of Desire

ANTHOLOGY
Wanting a Child
(coedited with Helen Schulman)

FICTION
The Life Room
House Under Snow

THE
SKIERS

SELECTED POEMS

Jill Bialosky

PUBLICATIONS
2010

Published by Arc Publications,
Nanholme Mill, Shaw Wood Road
Todmorden OL14 6DA, UK

Design by Tony Ward
Printed in Great Britain
by the MPG Books Group, Bodmin and King's Lynn

978 1904614 43 2 (pbk)
978 1904614 93 7 (hbk)

ACKNOWLEDGEMENTS

Grateful acknowledgment is made to the editors of the following publications, where poems in this volume first appeared:

(from *The End of Desire*) *The New Yorker, PN Review, TriQuarterly, Gulfstream, Agni Review, Pequod, Antioch Review, Partisan Review, International Poetry Review, Intro 14* and *Pavement*. 'Sisters' received the Elliott Coleman Award in Poetry, selected by Hugh Kenner, and was published in *Ellipsis*. 'Oh Giant Flowers' was nominated for a General Electric Foundation Award.

(from *Subterranean*) *Agni Review, American Poetry Review, American Diaspora: Poetry of Displacement (University* of Iowa Press), *The Nation, The New Republic, Open City, Paris Review, PN Review, Poetry, SunDog: Southeast Review, Tin House* and *Like Thunder: Poets Respond to Violence in America* (University of Iowa Press).

(from *Intruder*) *The Atlantic Monthly, Cortland Review, The Gettysburg Review, Harvard Review, Kenyon Review, Pequod, Salt* and *TriQuarterly*.

The author thanks Yaddo Corporation for the Arts, Ragdale Foundation and Virginia Center for the Creative Arts for their support of *The End of Desire*.

She also wishes to express her thanks and indebtedness to the following individuals for their help with the three collections from which poems in this volume have been selected: Jin Auh, David Baker, Catherine Barnett, Eavan Boland, Sarah Chalfant, the late Harry Ford, and Deborah Garrison.

Cover photograph by Pal Hermansen
by permission of Getty Images

Supported by
**ARTS COUNCIL
ENGLAND**

Arc International Poets: Editor: John Kinsella

For David and Lucas

CONTENTS

from INTRUDER

from
THE END OF DESIRE
(1997)

I was of three minds,
Like a tree
In which there are three blackbirds
        WALLACE STEVENS

FATHERS IN THE SNOW

In memory of Milton Abraham Bialosky

1.

The game is called father.

My sister lies in the grass.
I take handfuls of leaves
we raked from the lawn
spilling them over her body

until she's buried –

her red jacket lost, completely.
Then it's my turn.

Afterwards, we pick the brittle pieces
from each other's hair.

2.

After father died
the love was all through the house
untamed and sometimes violent.
When the dates came we went up to our rooms
and mother entertained.
Frank Sinatra's "Strangers in the Night,"
the smell of Chanel No. 5 in her hair and the laughter.
We sat crouched at the top of the stairs.
In the morning we found mother asleep on the couch
her hair messed, and the smell
of stale liquor in the room.
We knelt on the floor before her,
one by one touched our fingers
over the red flush in her face.
The chipped sunlight through the shutters.
It was a dark continent
we and mother shared;

11

it was sweet and lonesome,
the wake men left in our house.

3.

I'm not going to deny
the orange center of the flower
each last breath that passed
over the table
in the autumn gone away.

I wanted to take that afternoon
and put it in a safe place.
In a wooden box on the mantel
of a house I always imagine,
or in the hole I once dug
in the backyard for the imagined, stilled heart.

I wanted the day to stop
the way a movie would –
or to play it over in a place
my mind makes room for.

It was no large matter
of love, it was everything:
the grey afternoon, the Saturday
that began like a procession
inside a small flower
a young girl might tear apart.

4.

The day mother hammered closed
its silver door
we were outside
shaking the branches,

holding hands and dancing
in a circle around the tree.

Later, from the upstairs bathroom
we listened, three sisters taking turns.
One sister put her head
inside the laundry chute
that led through the deep tunnel
to the cellar,
called his name
and waited for the hollow echo
to answer back.

At night I faced the window,
my gold pillow, like a treasure,
pressed against my chest,
the giant tree spreading
over the house.

If I stared long enough
the branches would save me
from the voice of my father
trapped inside the chute.

5.

When the lightning
struck we were sure the dark limbs would splinter
but instead the tree was all light
and beautiful.
The tree long ago had been transformed,
had become for us, our father.

For days after the storm
we guarded its dark secret.
There were no blessings

large enough for that body
wrapped in weathered bark.

The day the men came
to cut down our tree
we had said them all:
One sister rubbed
her doll's face with mud
that covered the twisted roots,
the other sister hammered
her fist against the bark.

I carried a last leaf
in my pocket for luck.

6.

I come home
to the white framed house,
the paint on the side peeling
as if grieving for something lost

and the yellow forsythia tree
grown wild in the backyard
letting go its closed blossoms.

By the side door
is the milk chute
we crawled through
nights locked out of the house.

And in the backyard,
the stump of our oak tree
standing like a headstone
in the middle of the dried lawn.
Once its brown limbs protected our roof.

Indoors mother sleeps
all day on her double bed
while dandelions work their way
through the torn-up grass.

7.

Once there was a game the sisters liked to play
remembering mother at the vanity,
at five o'clock before the sun went down:
she dabbed perfume behind her ears,
in the crevice of her breasts.
The mirror lights illuminated her made-up face.
We even imitated the kiss she gave to father.

Then one day her ruby red lips,
mascara lashes, powdered cheeks
were veiled underneath black lace,
and on mother's pale face
we saw the colour, like a dead light, go out.

8.

It is old,
the jade, its thick leaves clean of dust;
I remember bringing the plant home
for mother's birthday.
Widowed, she thought the years had stopped.

I see her in the kitchen
washing dishes,
her dripping hand rubbed away
steam from the plate glass.

In the window the house plants
grown over, the dark vines tangled

like the knots she cut
with scissors from our hair.

My sisters and I were outdoors
building fathers out of snow.
We left her alone for hours,
our skin raw,
holding white like warmth in our hands.
She was almost invisible
in the icy air.

9.

It was the light of day
dispersing, the white light
of my mother's skin
and the light of her love
sparkling in the snow.
From the window
I saw her playing solitaire.
I had watched her play
so many nights
from outside I could feel
each card slapped down.
There was no escape
from the rash of her loss:
it was the cold rusty
taste of snow
I licked off my mitten;
the chill down my spine
when my sister
put her snow-filled hand
under my coat,
the other sister
holding me down;
it was those long dark shadows

I believed looked after us,
gigantic in the snow.

10.

Years ago I found them
scattered like dead leaves
in a suitcase in the basement:
the pictures of my father.

I took the best ones
time hadn't reached
and opened the edges
curled like a hand.

I put them in a shoe-box,
slipped under my bed.
It was like a secret
I imagined we shared.

Eventually the tint of age
faded the images,
erased the details.
Even my hands forgot you.

A SISTER'S STORY

My sister startles herself from sleep.
I can feel her breath rise
in the slow-motion of mine.
I am thirteen, and she is three.

Outside sleep unravels from our bodies.
Her hand, perfect for cradling a coin,
closes within mine.
We walk in the backyard

over long grass,
between weeping willow trees.
She won't remember her dream
so I tell her another:

How a girl alone in the night,
the stars so close to her,
she takes a pair of scissors
and cuts them from the sky.

She opens her slate-coloured book,
arranges the stars
into constellations,
pastes them flat as doilies.

They are like a billion
burning hearts.
Each morning the book
stretches back to the sky.

PREMONITION

I was wrapped in the darkest
part of sleep
when your cry broke through.

For a long time I lay there
waiting for mother
to cross from her room,

to lift her last born
from the fragments of your dream.
But she was hard into her sleep

where alcohol formed
its impenetrable cloud.
Inside your nursery

the air was humid
and safe
as a greenhouse.

I could see the moon
from the window
turning its back on the world.

I rocked you against my shoulder.
Sweat broke across the soft v
on the top of your forehead.

Your face was wet and warm.
The first fears
engraving your sleep.

MY MOTHER WAS A LOVER OF FLOWERS

I knew the kind that enchanted her:
a dozen weakened red and pink roses on our table.
Mother would remark how lovely and soft,
and bask in their aroma.
Once she was like a flower.
So beautiful that everyone wanted to know her.
Like a centrepiece, her aura said,
look, don't touch.

One autumn she brought home a bunch
of orange and yellow grotesquely shaped orchids.
Their petals resembled insects I had studied in biology.
She taught me that ugliness could be a form of beauty,
but I was afraid of it, of anything that captured her attention.
I saw what it did to one of us, her last born.

She liked to parade around our house
making sure each room was filled with flowers.
She made sure she had the right vase
so as not to clash with her bouquets;
for hours worked on her arrangements.
In the summer she loved lilacs,
in winter white roses, springtime a configuration of daisies.

Cut flowers live a short life.
Mother took them from the vase,
tied the stems with rope
and hung them upside down in a damp room
as if to preserve what she sacrificed.
That's how I learned I had no power
to stop nature from murdering beauty.

SISTERS

Opening the door I expect to find you there
tripping the steps, thin wing of hair
sweeping behind, the colour of half-ripened corn.

A welcome one dreams about, coming home from the seas or war.
This time I see you have changed.
Upstairs harbouring behind your door

the way we hid together behind books,
entered worlds we hadn't known, prairies we stumbled across,
little women, petticoats, herbal recipes,

secret gardens we believed were real, red barns,
horses that could make you cry, magic, painted roads.
The dark at the end of the forest sweating in your dreams.

Now inside your rooms parcels of childhood
arrange themselves like down quilted on your bed,
I carry them in my arms while you pull away.

I'm surprised finding your face thinned, diamond white,
eyes that pool tears so much like stars, the light behind them.
Your hair, like fallen leaves, dies a little more each day;

the colour is a suspension of yellow and brown.
Your small breasts float on your chest, are apple blossoms
bobbing in a pond. Your body wanders off like a shadow.

It all comes back, hurrying past every mirror,
giving in to that last trail of light, then in bed suspending
that moment in dreams of yourself, women you flip in magazines.

I want to make it all easy, or at least have answers
for the old body shed, for the new horrors
that arise at night, for parents quarrelling,

for friends turning away and returning daily,
for desires you can't name, longings for the ease of a dream,
answers I can't give you. Reasons for surviving the night.

THREE ON A MATCH

Summer nights we played gin rummy
in the backyard even when the mosquitoes
drove us crazy.
Our sister's hair had grown to the arch
of her back and she wore eyeliner,
black as lead, under her eyes.
As long as the lantern burned
we kept dealing the hands.
We were safe
in our protective net
of stars and constellations,
until one night she told us she was running away.
She had grown sick and tired
of the wind that ruffled the lilac bushes,
her small bedroom next to mother's
so close she could hear her breathe
through the walls,
and our childish gambling.
The night she came home
with suck bites covering her neck,
smelling of smoke and some boy,
I saw the change in her eyes,
and waited.
With one fatal sweep
she cleared away our pile of pennies,
took a twenty dollar bill
from the pocket of her jeans
and demanded we ante-up.
That's how it usually went:
she would call the game
and set the stakes,
and my younger sister and I would follow suit.
When I looked up the Big Dipper,
and the Little Dipper –
its sorry imitation –
were in the sky.

CAROUSEL

She came home drunk and laughing
with two boys from school.
I heard her footsteps coming down the stairs,
her hot breath in my ear
as she taunted me downstairs.
The night I let the other boy
feel me in the dark
my sister said it would be like heaven.
I followed down the linoleum stairs
to the damp cellar of the house.
Heaven, a place so far lost,
beyond fear and the pledge of higher virtue.
My sister twirled her long hair behind her ear,
her hoop earring
shining in the candlelight
was like the gold ring
in the centre of the carousel
we all wanted to touch,
the night turning, the music pumping
faster and faster.
When I felt his hand like a cold knife
under my shirt, I watched her polished nails
close around the other boy's neck
and leave their red marks.
Her spirit over me like the canopy
of the carousel's white blinking lights
I endlessly lost myself beneath.
When the music finished and the platform
of the room stilled, I couldn't stop him;
her reckless heart was mine.

RUINED SECRET

My sister fell in love
with an ex-con when she was seventeen
and swore me to secrecy.
I knew what she loved about him
the night she took me
to his run-down three family
on the dark side of a Cleveland
I'd never seen before.
On the top floor his mother lived
alone with twenty some cats
she called Sam.
From downstairs we could hear her
call the cats for dinner
and the sound of their twenty some
pairs of feet fill her kitchen.
When he heard his mother's voice
through the floorboards
he looked ashamed and lit
one of his non-filtered cigarettes
and told us the story of his brother
who was a captain in the Navy.
The smell of danger and lust
was everywhere –

in the sheets
crumpled on his bed,
in the small bathroom
wall-papered with rock stars,
the dirt underneath his nails;
his slow-tongued English of the streets.
At night my sister
talked to him on our princess phone
in the lemon-scented bedroom we shared
in whispers, and sighed at what I knew
were his hopeless declarations.

After six months the situation had changed.
My sister refused his phone calls,
and when a dozen red roses arrived,
she dumped them in the trash out back
before mother had gotten home.
Even though months had gone by
and we stopped saying his name,
his soft darkness lived in our room
like a ruined secret.

One day he waited for her after school
in his run-down Pontiac
and she came home with her eye
bruised and a pair of garnet earrings
in her ears.

She did not know how to get rid
of what she started.
He went to his priest
to ask for salvation
and later that same day
when I was working
at the bakery counter after school
he took me by the arm,
cried, and begged me to forgive him.
In our bedroom we stared at the phone
waiting for the scary thrill
that pumped through our bodies
after the first ring;
but eventually the calls stopped
and I'd find my sister
staring out the window
turning the scarlet posts
on her ear that caught
the light like a bleeding heart.

STAIRWAY TO HEAVEN

My girlfriend and I snuck out
of our houses at midnight
on a Cleveland winter night
and met at the corner of our block.
Our mission was to find the two gas station
attendants we had spotted the night before.
We didn't know their names,
only their oily hands and dark coats.
Marie had big boobs and soft, Czech lips.
I was a quiet teenager with slight curves
and deep, skirting eyes.
We were a sensible team:
she was the target and I was the protection.
One boy was cuter than the other,
that's how it always went.
Marie would get in the back seat
and neck with the cute one
and I'd stay in front pressed against
the passenger door talking to the gawky driver
with a scar underneath his eye or bad teeth
above the sound of "Stairway to Heaven" or something
by Fleetwood Mac, until their lips in the back
were bruised and puffy.
Eventually, the driver pulled over
and let us out at the curb.
Marie scribbled her phone number on a matchbook.
For two or three days we'd linger near the phone
until pissed-off and pumped with revenge
we'd go out again, stalking the night
for the new replacements.
This time was my turn, I decided.
Outside the Sohio
we leaned against the unleaded
and waited for their shift to end.

When we got to the car
I slipped in the back,
Ignoring Marie's tug on my sleeve.
The good one slipped in next.
The tape began: "Lucy in the Sky with Diamonds,"
joint lit, and within minutes
we were in the haze of music and drug
until we'd open the door
and let the cold blast of air rescue us.
His name was Randy.
The very minute the words slipped
from his lips I didn't want to forget him.
Randy, I thought, over and over
as he turned a lock of my hair
in his finger and began his work.
No, I liked the smell of petroleum
on his neck, his nicotine lips.
I could make him up in my mind
for weeks, I thought, without
knowing a single thing about him.
This time we'd wait by my phone
and when it rang I'd say, Randy,
Hello. Two words.
And the long dark dialogue
would begin.

MY GROOM

It was almost religious,
watching my groom carry out his ritual:
filling the pails with water,
coffee can with dried corn and oats
and emptying the grain into deep troughs.
I would vow to forget him
and then, not wanting to, it would happen,
I would return each year
to the open fields of Ohio
where he ran the racehorses,
the golden light of autumn
beating against their dark manes.
After the races, we'd go back to the barn
to the horses banging against their cramped stalls,
snorting and sneezing, wanting to break loose.
I watched him cool the horses down,
the flies everywhere,
my groom, his long arms taut
under his T-shirt as he carefully
brushed their backs, coaxed,
cleaned the open welts on their legs
where he'd whipped them into shape.
His fingernails were caked with mud,
long hair slicked off his forehead with sweat.
From the corner of the barn
light weakened in the slats of the roof,
bats screeched in the eaves.
When he finished he'd look at me,
standing in the shadows.
Up close, I smelled the horses,
dark and dangerous, wedded to his clothes.
His warm hands slipped down my back
underneath my shirt;
horse hooves wild as my heart
against the earth's secrets.
Is this where love begins,
in the arms of the cruel tamer,
the keeper of horses?

OH GIANT FLOWERS

Everyday I walk past the house
with the blue morning glories
covering the walls and the four sunflowers

growing in front, their tall stalks
bent over, and have to stop
and touch the dark centres

almost the size of a face.
It began the morning I awoke before you.
The blanket was wrapped tightly around you

and the sun came through the window
on your face. I couldn't stand
to see you that way. I looked outside.

The leaves red, yellow, and finishing.
A squirrel was in the yard rummaging for food
in the grass, the apple tree letting go

its bruised fruit; preparations had to be made.
How could you sleep with so much sun on your face?
When I left I didn't know where I was going.

There was so much colour it seemed as if the whole
sky would ignite. The light loves the earth so much
it has to burn to prove it. Oh giant flowers,

when I came across you I wanted to bury my face
in your huge petals, I wanted to lie down
in the grass beneath you.

WITHOUT

Why does the woman lay her head so far
against her shoulder, why the still smile?
Her blouse only covers one of her breasts
and her plump arms are milky white.
Perhaps she has just made love, dressed,
and moved to the red chair after her lover
has left. Her hands are placed
over her crotch but it is not pain that draws
her face, or if so, pain cut small by pleasure.
In the hour after she held on to him the way
she must have been held as a young girl
before she had begun to bleed.
Already one side of her face is darkening.
Later she might cut her yellow hair.
She is without her lover and her father
is far away. Her face is the halves of a heart.

IRONING

The girl is ironing in the small
light left after dusk.
Her head tilted over the board,
her long red hair almost catching in the iron.
She sprinkles water from a blue bowl
onto a printed shirt.
Light steam slowly escapes.
Already her eyes look older.
She remembers as a child watching her mother
pressing the sheets. She helped fold them,
asking questions one after another,
listening to the sound of her mother's voice.
All that mattered was that the sheets
were cold and crisp when she slipped into bed
and smelled like the wind that blew them dry.
Now she slides the iron down the back of the shirt and yawns.
She belongs to no one.

WHAT YOU ARE LEFT WITH

When the summer leaves
it takes some light

with it. Some birds go
too. All the windows

have to be closed.
The cold comes

and you live with it.
The trees lose

their leaves but
the branches are still strong

and suffice. The wind goes
on. But in your mind

you still hold the birds,
the green grass

and the red tomatoes
weighing down the vine.

SKATING POND

The grey sky gives over
and the dark starlings gather
in one otherwise empty tree.
The bleachers are cold.

No one is skating
but deep scratches
are gouged in the ice.

It is enough to look out
past the pond where certain trees
and houses alter
simply by the raw snow
falling in the January light.

The sun spreads itself to nothing
and the day holds on
to what little is left.
And because you don't know
what you want, all of it matters.

COLD HEART

The slow drift of clouds
neglects the face of the sun,
and the snow keeps coming.

The less than tame wind dismantles it,
brushes the black branches
of a particular oak to one side
like a girl throwing back her hair.
The ice engraved in the crevices
of bark is your idea of sensual.

You would find it more than beautiful,
this wilderness where a pine
is the only thing in sight, green, unstripped.
Only you'd be obsessed with the lesser,
barer trees, how immense you'd feel
next to them, how gracious you'd become,

and the starlings, how they regroup
from tree to tree in one thick flock,
how they leave not one alone.
Sometimes the wind gets so crazy
and goes on for so long,
as though confessing

to the air. You would stand still and listen,
note how the dry falling snow
dies into the rest of itself,
and for a minute your cold heart

would quiver. I wish you could see
each morning the red-headed woodpecker
knocking against the bark,
how safe he is from all reasoning.

SNOW FALLING UPSIDE DOWN

The sound of the chamber organ
came into my life
the way the snow might have fallen
over a red glove I found one March morning
when everything had begun to thaw.

Two or three stars
broke the complete
sky and the brave ash stood

33

silvered and still in the loneliness
of the air.

The wind sighed its long
regret against the window
of the thrift shop –
the music's crescendo
falling over the antique doll
no one could hold,

and beside her the paperweight,
where a snowman inside a globe
holds a yellow balloon in his hand.
If you turned the globe upside down
it was as if his world were breaking apart,
and the balloon, like a lost heart
in the snow, eventually drifted away.

HISTORY LESSON

This is the way we learn history:
how each grass blade breathes
until the entire lawn shifts,
or the way we remember a certain friend
by the way she tore leaves from trees,
or our mother rubbing silver
for the table at dusk.

Last night over coffee
my friend's voice defined regret,
he no longer spoke with his hands.
He said sadness was the way
autumn trees gave up their leaves
as he watched the movers stack boxes
outside his parents' home;

how his father never forgave him
for refusing to go to war.

The year I turned thirteen
I couldn't stand any of them.
Once a year we used to gather for the holiday
around grandmother's table,
my mother, sisters, aunts, uncles, cousins;
It was the taste of challah, soft and doughy
that I remember.
The dining-room was too hot;
my grandfather ate with his fork turned around;
grandmother's wet kisses.

All that day, like a fool
I thought it was possible to disown my family.
I listened impatiently to the story
of how my great-grandmother in Russia
braided bread for the evening meal,
lit candles, softened the white flame with her hands
and whispered the ancient prayer for bread,
dark wine, for all of us, even the unborn.

SILVER

On the butcher block table
is the silver that has been housed
in a moulded cardboard box in mother's basement
and handed down to me as my inheritance.
It was great grandmother's silver;
she died in Russia before I was born.
From great grandmother's table
this silver came to rest in another
drawer in the cherry bureau
of her daughter's house in Cleveland.

It came to me as I began my work.
This silver had been set, and washed,
and laid down again, night after night,
with bowls of borscht, roasted potatoes,
brisket so tender it could be cut with a fork,
in the evening candlelight after the Sabbath.
It was this butter knife
my father held in his hand, and raised
against his father in anger.
This fork he eagerly
brought to his lips
as he listened to the hushed talk
of babies lost and relatives killed in the war.

It took all day to polish the serving for twelve,
the salt and pepper shakers, sugar bowl, and creamer
all wearing the monogrammed inscription
of the family initial.
Afterwards I was tired.
I looked at my days work spread out on the butcher block,
sparkling against the last stain of sun
the way one might come upon
a dark family secret
rubbed out after a month,
a year, a decade of tarnish.

THE DAY THE WORLD STOPPED

The day the world stopped
I was lying on my bed
on a muggy Saturday afternoon.
The wind so still it was as if the world,
like a baby born too soon, had just taken its last breath.

In the house next door someone's mother
was chopping onions and cabbage for slaw.
Was it for a picnic at the lake,
a family barbecue?
From the house behind us
I could hear our neighbour working on his car,
the sound of each tool as it hit the hot pavement.

I have always admired the art of keeping house,
the clickety-clack of dishes being stacked,
the growl of the garbage disposal sucking up
the last trace of a graceful dinner
laboured over all day.
The ordinary rhythms of a house
untouched by anguish.

It was so quiet
you could hear the sprinklers on the lawn
roll in their perfect arcs.
If there is a sound the heart makes when it breaks
it wasn't heard.

THE END OF DESIRE

When I was a child
I used to love to stare at lovers –
at couples kissing, a man looking
longingly into a woman's eyes,
a woman adoring back
and marvel over the possibilities of love.
Usually I was with my sister,
standing in a grocery line,
or outside a theatre.
She would tug at my sleeve,
roll her eyes and banish me with her words:

"Stop staring! What's wrong with you!"
I did feel that something was wrong –
that I could be so content absorbing
the wave of her hair, the scent of perfume,
his strong fingers cupped around her shoulder.
It was the long, uninterrupted gaze I most preferred.
At the movies, I would draw into myself
as I watched on the big screen lovers kiss
and felt a stab of pain in the centre of my stomach
travel through my body like a drug –
and for that brief time it was as though
I was the lover, the receiver of such rapt attention.
When the lights came on I carried the kiss
with me all through the rest of the late afternoon,
through the long walk home underneath the autumn arbors,
through the dull and tedious routine of dinner,
until I was alone in my bedroom and could replay
the scene in my mind without interruption.
I knew that as long as I was allowed to look,
to linger, to stare,
to become one with that spell that was so other,
to know and then to have –
that one day, my desire would end.

THE DROWNING

It isn't human not to struggle
underwater

not to want to breathe.
Yesterday at our neighbour's pool

you forced my head underwater,
a game to see who could stay under longest,

who could suffer longer.
When I started to rise up for air

you pulled my shoulders down,
wanting to see me struggle.

My legs and arms flailed,
then instinctively

I kicked you until I surfaced.
At night you reach for me

in our bed,
slide into my back,

brush your lips
against my forehead, eyes, face

as if you've really saved me,
and are overcome with remorse

for what you nearly lost,
a tenderness a small child,

a woman who has not been loved
in years, a damaged sister,

would covet.
Harder, I say, be mean.

The way I learned to love
was to give, to be kind, patient,

to be not someone to fight for.
When I close my eyes

I'm still floating
face down

waiting for you
to breathe air into my lungs.

What I want is to defy
my nature.

Stronger, I say.
Make it stop,

the desire.
Hurt me, I say, harder.

THE RUNAWAY

On a summer day full of promise
we piled into my mother's car
and drove my youngest sister
to camp for the summer.

That night she ran away
and called from a stranger's
house to beg our mother
to bring her home.

Years later,
she took the keys
to my mother's white Saab,
closed the garage door
and turned on the ignition.

On a day less remembered
for the violent rain
than for how little was the same as before,
the sky closed its eyes on our house
as if in shame and claimed her.

THE SUICIDE'S GARDEN

In her garden
tall and sleek roses grow decadently

for the shears, and for our pleasure.

Look how lovely
the fresh cut roses on my table.

Their life so short,
and yet no less beautiful

or real, than the roses
on the vines in the garden.

How willingly the tender
prepares the earth for beauty's sake:

as if he were the master of her execution.

THE GODDESS OF DESPAIR

Against such cold and mercurial mornings,
watch the wind whirl one leaf
across the landscape,
then in a breath, let it go.
The colour in the opaque sky
seems almost not to exist.

Put on a wool sweater.
Wander in the leaves,
underneath healthy elms.
Hold your child in your arms.

After the dishes are washed,
a kiss still warm at your neck,
put down your pen. Turn out the light.

I know how difficult it is,
always balancing and weighing,
it takes years and many transformations;
and always another loss to stop for,

to send you backwards.

Why do you worry so,
when none of us is spared?

STOLEN CRY

I awoke at two a.m.
and looked out the bay windows
as the pregnant sky gradually came to life.

From the backdrop of weathered buildings
I heard a cry in the night.
The sound of something injured.
The nursery was empty.

A greedy lover,
to give to his betrothed,
had robbed us of what was promised.

AMERICAN LANDSCAPE

The tern dives headfirst into the sea,
catches a fish, soars again, takes another dive.
There is not a rusted can, cigarette butt,
Big Mac wrapper on the beach.
The ocean stretches like a canvas
to the edge of the pale pastels of this artificial
mini beach town city designed by an architect
I heard Prince Charles had praised.

Modern steel sculptures in the shape of sea birds
appear to have landed on front lawns,
hand-painted Santa Fe style furniture sits in living rooms
dotted swiss curtains and frilly fabrics
mimic scenes from story-books.
In this American city ten years old
everything is pre-arranged, pre-fabricated.
City planners and architects have come to study it.
I hear they are planning one in Maryland.

The beach is dotted with the delicate
thread-work of nests like clumps of tangled hair
and wears the imprint of the sandpipers,
their bellies the colour of sand.
The baby sandpipers have hatched.

In the air is the sound of their squeaking.
The monarchs have magically emerged from their cocoons.
There is no sign of humanity in sight.

It is like a ghost town now that it is October
and the second-home residents have migrated
back to their homes in Alabama, Missouri, Georgia.
I walk the Seaside, Florida streets
reading the names of the houses –
Châtelet, Peek-a-boo, Blue Moon.
One of the twenty-six year round residents
remarked that in this town the gossip
is about other people's houses.

THE DAWN OF THE END
OF CIVILIZATION

I carry the image like a treasured snapshot:
a lovely man dressed in a soft, faded sweatshirt,
blue jeans, pair of flip-flops, carries his two year old red-head
boy in his arms across the small sand-pebbled roads
in a Disneyland-like town, Seaside, Florida,
where the houses are all pastels; on the last day of October,
headed toward the windy surf of a desolate beach
where only the rich have worn the shores barefoot
on sand fine as baby powder.
My boy would have been a red-head.

It was the eve of the first of November.
There was absolutely no sun. No chance.
Barely a slice of blue in the white opaque sky.
There was good food – salmon peppered and grilled.
Complicated conversation.
Later I walked the beach and shooed away flies.
The seductive, dangerous curl of the waves threatened to shake it,
but the image stayed with me. It was the dawn of the day
I would never give birth to; the life I would never have.

I was afraid.

from
SUBTERRANEAN
(2001)

*While wandering in the well-tended gardens,
she had innocently picked a pomegranate
from a dropping branch, and had placed in her
mouth seven seeds taken from its pale husk.*

OVID, *Metamorphoses*

SUBTERRANEAN

She did not know when it would happen
or how it would overtake her
or whether she would allow herself.
All I know is that she could not take it any more
lying day after day underneath the hollow tree, waiting,
consumed by a kind of fire,
wondering if there is a type of love
that saves us or whether there was more
to the world than the familiar paradise
of her mother's complicated and vivid garden.
She smelled nectar in the laboured-over
chrysanthemum and amaryllis,
but could not taste it.
I know if it were a flower it would have bloomed
in the cumulus overhead
void of volition and sin,
translucent as the filmy underside of a leaf.
If it were an animal she would have followed it,
but it was amorphous as feeling, weightless as dust,
turbulent as an entire undisclosed universe
radiating from the inner core beneath the earth
and, still, she longed for it.
Restless, she wandered from the elm
to the school-yard to smother an intensity
she could not squelch or simmer.
The wind swooned. Cement cracked. Deep into the underbelly
light travelled, no one in sight but his immense shadow,
and then a figure appeared out of the imagined dream
and matched it. So powerful, not for who he was
but for how her mind had magnified him
like a bug underneath cool glass,
every antenna and tentacle aquiver.
No sign of where she had been
or she came from. Only knowledge
that it would never be re-created
except by this: putting words down on a page
and that she had forever compromised
the joy of summer for a dismal, endless winter.

And as the field of force gathered,
raping every last silvery bough,
tantalizing each limb,
she forgot *even* the feel of herself.
When it was over she felt moisture. Rain.

FLIRTATION

On the shocking-pink shag carpet we lit incense, smoked joints,
read passages aloud from Nietzsche and Kierkegaard, just to see
how far we could go. We conducted séances, moved our hands along
the pilot of the Ouija board, invited our boyfriends up for sex,
took acid, experimented with mushrooms, got stoned on Quaaludes.
My first friend shot herself with a pistol. Seared in my brain
is her blue-and-white-gingham dress, knock knees and ankle socks
trimmed with a neat border of lace from our first grade class picture.
We played Barbies underneath the dim alcove in her room
while her mother, paralysed from a stroke, traversed the downstairs
in her wheelchair, Maraschino cherries floating in a Manhattan
cocktail on her tray, chain-smoking.
When we pulled ourselves away from the complex drama
in Barbie's Dream House and walked down the staircase
there was a fog so thick in the room we could barely see her.
Why Jeannie and not me? Why her and not Nancy or Ava
or Joanie or Jessica? Why her and not you, dear reader?
The one who mastered the flirtation,
the dead girl, she is the person I remember
when I long to travel further, to see underneath.

TERMINAL TOWER

From the top of the tower when the sun set in the Cuyahoga's
brown waters (the river caught fire to make our city the laughing stock
of a nation) it cast a dark shadow over the industrial sky.
To the Van Sweringen brothers it was like the Eiffel Tower of Paris
conceived in 1925 like a favourite child in a family – it foreshadowed
Rockefeller Center and gave to our city the second-tallest building –
to us it was grand as Mount Olympus.
It was the place we imagined Zeus and his cronies conducted
their mortal business. There is a legend about a lost daughter
and a mother who must bargain for her return. Weren't we all lost
inside our daydreams and imaginings? Didn't all of us
who lived off the shores of Lake Erie want to be claimed?
On an overcast day you can still make out the intricate
masonry of its patrician face. It was where the fathers
of our community worked, riding the rapid transit from the safe
suburbs through the poverty of the ghetto into the underbelly
of downtown. When we looked from the ground to the top
of the tower we felt our spirits elevate. Then I heard it, inside the crowds,
the honking of automobiles and shriek of an ambulance,
the singular cry, and he was there in all his omnipotence and I knew
my fate was locked inside the mortar of his mercurial façade
like wet leaves pressed into a mosaic on the pavement.
In synagogue we learned about Moses climbing the mount
and God's deliverance of the commandments. Whether the sound
came from a wounded gull or a school of dirty pigeons did not matter.
Whether it was Zeus or God the Almighty or my own vision
of my lost father was irrelevant.
It was the idea of being greater than myself I coveted. It was terminal,
the longing. It was magnificent, a tower that did not look desolate
in its setting, a structure to provide an anchor to the observer's glance,
a relief from the flatness of the world around us.
In the tower's square men clad in overcoats carrying briefcases
trafficked the street, rode its fifty-two floors to politick.
And it was at the very top where Zeus might have bargained
with the prince of the underworld for his daughter's return.
As I looked up the sweep of the tower's long elegance,
I saw through a mass of smog that I might lose myself forever
or I might survive.

I saw that he was looking after me, but that he was also indifferent.
I saw that love was fickle and adulterous and still I longed for him.
I saw that he betrayed us and that he could not save me.
I saw through the stone into the abyss. It was dark and splendid.

TORTURE

I

It was very cold
the long walks
we took.

The orange glow
of a fire in a window,
yellow gourds on a table;

red flames of those
autumn leaves
spiking the streets

with colour.
We walked.
We walked.

What else was there
but our walks.
One foot

in front
of the other.

Mice inhabited
our walls,
we heard them

scratching at night
and the sound
of their little feet

running from one wall
to another.
Rarely did they make

their presence known
beyond the walls
though once

on bed rest
with my first child
two mice slipped

between the splinter
of light
underneath the door

and the floor in the closet
where we stored
our wool coats

and ancient
vacuum cleaner
and dashed

across the floor.
A fear
I harboured

all those months
looked me square
in the eyes.

III

Our upstairs
neighbours are wrapped
in that cocoon

a baby brings
into a house.
No one enters.

No one gets
between them,
warmth drifts

down to us,
seeps
into the cracks.

IV

To stave off
loneliness
I took in two cats

for the company
not knowing
the female

was expecting.
I was in love
with a man

who lived
with another
woman.

He came to me
only in daylight
in the hours

between
my waitressing
shifts.

The steel sky,
cold, mercurial.
From my window

I saw the shame
in his face
as he walked up

the back
staircase,
watched

the shade
fall over it
when he turned

the lock
to my door
leaving

one woman,
entering the house
of another.

While we made love
in my twin bed

we could hear

the mother cat
turn in the drawer
where she had gone

to give birth.
The sound,
it was agony.

The flip-flops,
the thud,
thud, thud.

One she turned
her back on.
Why was the kitten sick?

Why did she refuse
to nurse it?
Was her death

preordained?
After we buried
her still wet

from the after-
birth,
and not the nurturing

rough tongue
of her mother,
a black, wet thing

no larger
than the palm
of my hand,

he came for me
but the sound
of his footsteps

on the warped
wood step
were weightless.

The sky vacant
of light
by then.

It was winter.
The Formica counters
cold.

My sheets,
the unsanded floors,
unbearably cold.

v

Another's
happiness
quiets me.

The image
of our neighbour
so tired from

interrupted sleep,
every day wired
she forgets

to change
her clothes,
wash her hair.

Day bleeds
into night,
light

bleeds
into the carpet.

VI

I had no stomach
for the traps
the super set

in our closet,
the kind with glue
where a mouse

would step into it
for a rectangle of cheese.
I couldn't bear

that kind of torture.

VII

Afterwards, the dry cleaner,
the Korean greengrocer,
the place

we went for croissants,
were forbidding
without the child

I had already
ingratiated
inside the white

space of my future,
already a mother
snaring her child

against her will.

VIII

That winter
was like one long
night.

I curled
against the wall
beside the bed

and turned
inward.
By then

there was no baby
to bring home
and we could no longer

live in the place
she was conceived.
The white walls.

The window seat
I lay in
from two to three

o'clock each day
for that sliver
of sun—

by April

we were gone.
It can happen.

When I hear
our neighbour's
footsteps

walking
back and forth
above us

to calm the colic
I remember
the window seat.

It is burned
there
in that slab

of light.
Behind
our walls,

I felt life move.

INTERIOR WITH CHILD

I

I walked
the erratic
jumble

of streets
in the middle

of the afternoon,

still a refuge
from my life,
and ducked

into a museum
to see it,
the grief

and mourning
art is wrought
from.

II

The children
followed.
One bruised

her knee,
another cried
out.

Tripped.
They walked
into the Renaissance

rooms
like a line
of quiet

civilized
soldiers.
You could hear

the sighing
of their sneakers
on the stone floors.

III

A girl
not unlike
the image

I formulated
of my own
daughter

reached down
to pull up
her knee socks

bunched
at her ankles.
A boy shot

a rubber band.
In the silent
corridors

connecting
one gallery
to the other

they giggled.
In their eyes
burned

the desire
to flee
the stale,

trapped air
and enter
the living

breathing
park they glimpsed
through glass.

IV

In the still world
filled
with porcelain

statues,
girls with pearl
earrings

and shuttlecock
and details
of the Virgin

and Child
painted in gold,
I heard a child

call out.
It was August.
Out our brownstone

window
the morning
glories—

their petals
closing at dusk
like the lips

of a child
over her mother's
breast—

climbed
the soot-dirt
walls.

SHADOW LIFE

I

In that quick-
silver
of time

between sleep
and waking,
the pitter-

patter
of footsteps
like rain

against a roof
penetrates
the membrane

of our dreams.
Half asleep,
the gravity

of a child's
body
presses up

against mine.
The stars outside
dissolve.

II

I studied
by day
and at night

gathered my
tips
in the pocket

of my waitress
apron
and shared my bed

with a boy
who later
went mad.

In the blue-grey
of that winter
conceived

on the rumpled
sheets of our bed
or in the midst

of dream
there was a child
between us,

the embryonic
nut floating
lost and unattached.

III

In the window-
less cellar
we touched

but never once
spoke
of what inextricably

bound us
like winter's
shadow.

All those nights
we held
each other

to keep
from floating
adrift,

lit
a candle
in the pitch

black,
and waited
until the moon

completed
its inevitable
course

and the candle
burned itself out.

IV

Surely the daffodils
have begun
to show

their yellow
crowns,
lifted,

a white frost
like a sheet
over the lawn,

the whirling
crescents
from the mobile

colliding
with the shadow
life in a boy's

room
when hot
with fever

he calls out
and doesn't
know me.

V

The snow
is wet
like rain.

It will not
stick
or accumulate

snuffing
out the colour
like the winter

the snow
fell so heavy
and uncompromising

I barely made it
to work,
the light

so oppressive
I craved
the crush

of darkness,
the return
to the mildewed

and damp
underworld
already let

to strangers.

VI

As he tromps
through
snow

up to his boot tops
to fetch
some twigs

for arms,
I remember
winter's

triumph:
shock
of newly fallen

snow
burning
into the ground

like memory,
his insistent
pair of tracks

from one side
of the yard
to the other,

the blinding
translucent
face

of a boy
carving out
holes

so the snow-
man
we've built

can see.

FOUR VERSIONS OF RAIN

I

Sky
half-mast,
grey,

long winter
dragging,
ground broken,

birds barely
awake.
The leaves

in shatters.
An evergreen
pulled up

from its roots
un-
tethered

blows
this way
and that

across
the field.

II

Underneath
the dim light
of the library

carrel,
the rain

battering

its frail
apology
against the window,

I remember
the boy
I knew

just out
of childhood.
Not a hint

of sun
on the naked
hill. Only

grass, shrub.
Face-to-face
in the waiting room

I wondered
where he had gone,
that boy,

would I find
him again?
On the hospital

bed
on top
of those white

stark sheets
I once
held him.

III

She is by
the windowsill,
the side

of a shingled house,
stubbornly
carrying a bucket

of sand,
a figment
more alive

than the rain
softening
the newly

sodded grass.
Rain stops.
Starts again.

Mud slips
and slides.

IV

After
the torrential
downpour

the sky
impartial
to the emerging

light,
I hear them
talking

in the kitchen,
the tink, tink,
tink

of their silver
spoons
against porcelain,

my son's teeth
crunching
his Cheerios,

and listen
(the rain
now a drizzle).

When I bend
down to tie
his shoe—

his first pair
embalmed
in bronze—

I think,
don't hold on
so tight,

let him go.

MYSTERY

Out of darkness came chaos
and from chaos there was a child.
A daughter.
Hair the colour of wheat and tarnish.
There was a great bed
like a calm lake you wanted to float along
on your back all day
and dream of a world untouched
by discord and violence.
A world entirely whole and sane
and unlacking,
where above in the mysterious sky
you could chart order in the stars
and constellations.
It was a mother's bed,
no less, and at night the child in her own
pictured the world her mother entered
after the bath had been drawn,
the last light extinguished,
when she returned to her cool sheets.
She imagined the surface sleek and frozen
like a thick layer
of ice
a child might scratch her skates on
and, underneath it, brooding and forbidding waters
and then the ice cracked,
heaven and earth divided
and her mother fell into open arms.
And when dawn came she'd had enough.
There was quiet.
There was no weeping.

THE WRATH OF THE GODS

She walked to the back
of the hot bus, queasy from the smell
of gasoline, past the place where boys congregated,
checking out each girl who dared to pass
the unspoken initiation
to the tiny bathroom
suffocating as a confessional
to discover for the first time its dark stain.
After the raucous pounding (the boys beating on the door)
quieted, she emerged into the dim light
but nothing had changed.
No boy later that night slipped into the empty seat
to whisper in her ear.
No girls flocked around her to share
in the newfound glory.
If there were gods, they were sent here
for one purpose, to decree that out of abundance
was pain, and from suffering
perhaps one day a child.
At the top of the monument
that brought them on the journey
early that day, tired after their triumph
(eight hundred and ninety-seven stone steps!),
she knew she was at the edge
of something grand and momentous
where she could see the glimmer –
the Lincoln and Thomas Jefferson Memorials
and our nation's Capitol, the dotted figures
of lovers strolling in the park,
the cherry trees in blossom! –
of what lay beyond
the guarded, serpentine walls
of her suburban community
where she might one day
forge her independence.
On the mount she could feel the press
of sun anointing her face, the air
like joy, building inside her;

the presence of our founding fathers
no longer imposed its dense weight.
But it wasn't until her mother picked her up
at the high school in the twilight
after the journey
that she knew no one
(perhaps not even the gods)
was watching.
The stars trembled.
The restless moths went at the streetlamp.
In the yard crickets screeched.
Twigs snapped.
The red, poisonous berries
from the tree shading her driveway
shed on the windshield of their car.

MUSIC LESSON

I thought I was like her.
I would have sung, played the violin, piano, flute,
made music my life's work. I could hear the rapture;
the sound of the metronome as we stood straight,
chin up, heels of our Mary Janes
and loafers against the wood step.
Sometimes on the way to school,
I felt a melody build in the cave
of my body like a sudden
brightness just before letting go.
In assembly we stood in tiers depending
on our height as if we were the chorus
on the steps of the Theatre of Dionysus
looking into the hollow stage
in anticipation of a great tragedy.
We followed the tempo
against the movement of our maestro's stick,

watched the O of her lips
as she mouthed the words. I concentrated.
I let the air fill my diaphragm
just as she instructed.
Once I looked away from her
and turned, just a quick glimpse, to look at him.
Like Narcissus, he would have found a pool,
a lake, his image in the glass of the music room's window
and looked at his reflection all day. Still,
like a love-struck nymph (I was only a child)
I liked to watch.
To feel the light brush of his breath
on the back of my neck as he sang.
My country 'tis of thee
sweet land of liberty
of thee I sing;
land where our fathers died…
I sang louder, inhaling the air
and allowing it to sail through my being
until it was no longer me but the notes
of a beautiful bird dispatched
of her doom to echo the same notes
who had at last found her voice.
But it was too late.
In that one glance of betrayal
she saw inside the hidden chamber
my true self inhabited
and deemed to silence it.
My teacher looked at me
and put her index finger over her stern lips.
I never sang again. I was quiet.

THE FATE OF PERSEPHONE

I THE VOW

It is always winter.
The fields always
cold and brittle.

The barren trees
white as a shroud.
The night screams.

When I was full of her,
corn, wheat, fruits
of the orchard,

flourished. Now
I live without light.
I refuse to be

in the company
of the divine
without my daughter.

Wasted leaves
drown in the birdbath;
the statue in the garden

casts her eyes.

II THE CURSE

Once she tore
the narcissus from the garden
(the shaft of sunlight

must have prematurely
drawn her gaze)
like a girl too eager

76

for love
she was plunged back
untethered

never to breathe again.
She kicked and screamed
but no one

(not even her mother
who raped the earth
in grief)

heard her nocturnal cries.

III THE PLOT

They were brothers.
One lived for immortality
the other for seduction.

When the one who ruled
saw that his own daughter
was the token

of his brother's affection,
still he did not intervene,
or if he did,

it was with one caveat:
if she tasted
the fruit,

she would bear
the curse
of her desire.

IV The Fruit

The ancient black
cherry trees
and the graffiti

of their gnarled
limbs imprint
their shadow.

There at the juncture
of lawn and meadow
the crêpe myrtle bark

peels to a new
cinnamon colour.
Still in the autumnal

haze,
the berry-berry
shrub,

still young, still vibrant
drops bright, violent
violet berries

as if in penance
for what the earth
must suffer.

THE CIRCLES, THE RINGS

I don't think it was snowing
the afternoon the child tied the long laces of her skates
together, hung them over her shoulder, and trudged
through the snow to the lake where they skated
so she would not be persuaded to roam
the forgotten plains lusting after boys,
committing unredeemable acts – self-flagellation,
starvation, promiscuity – tortured
by the blooming sense of brilliance
the flower of her youth had driven through her like a stake,
so that when she skated she was light
as a leaf blown toward the winds of heaven.

I don't think it was snowing
the late afternoon the child carved out
with her blades the nine rings and followed their course
as if lured from error, her scarf tangled
in her hair, so lost in the momentum of thrust and dig,
glide, glide, glide, that she dodged past other skaters without a glance.
The bodies of boys pushed into her, spun her, nearly slammed
her to the frozen ground, but still she skated on
crossing over into the shaded realm, further
into the subterranean depths as if in pursuit of a saviour.

I don't think it was snowing
the moment she sensed there was no Beatrice
to lead her from folly, nor a guide as passionate or kind
as a poet to accompany her, and though she would have longed
to converse with Homer or Ovid, only the forest of incantations
from the Inferno unveiled their terrible fates.
Daylight turned to dusk and she skated in the dampness
consumed in a whirlwind as if confronted by the judge of the damned.
The hot dogs turned on the wheel, the sweet smell of hot chocolate
from the concession filled the gluttonous air,
a pair of skaters circled obsessively in the figure eight
as if entrapped in a state of limbo, but she skated on
transfixed by the dizzying power of her motion.

I don't think it was snowing
when she took the third and fourth circles past girls
decked in furs and fancy hats, girls who were prettier, smarter, craftier –
how many hours had she daydreamed about their lives?
As they sped past, she saw the weakness of their eyes, the frailty
of their smiles, how their once beautiful bodies had gone to waste.
Around the fifth circle she swept past the clashing cacophony of boys
on their hockey skates, sticks in hand, warring against each other,
forsaking, now that the sun had fallen, the yellowness
of its eternal gaze.

I don't think it was snowing
when the rebellious guards who stood watch
in front of the Iron Gates brought out the stretchers
and whipped past to help those who had fallen
and would not let her pass. It wasn't until the furies
descended and threatened to white out the landscape
that she heard the voice over the loudspeaker,
as if it were the messenger from heaven warning
the skaters to change direction, and watched the guards
carrying the mangled bodies of the children, that she recalled
how she once denied the dead immortality
and while the snow began to fall
she stood and prayed.

I don't think it was snowing
having minutes before blanketed the ice (it must have stopped)
when she circled the seventh ring, the ice choppy as rock
as she glided over the river of blood and nearly crashed
into two skaters stopped in a brawl and listened to their angry
accusations. She recalled the time she stole and lied, arguments
with her sisters, how she forsook one friend for another,
the guilt she bore for surpassing the beauty of her mother.
If it were snowing it might have penetrated
the dried grass and broken roots,
it might have fallen like a wet rain onto her hair,
she might have been seduced
by its coppery glitter.

I don't think it was snowing
as she made the round of the seventh circle,
crossing one skate over the other, when she heard
in the air the chilling voices of the lost suicides
call out to her as if they were encased
in the triumphant branches of the trees
whose leaves were long ravished and winded.
In the forest beyond woodpeckers
went at the bodies of the trees; birds
shrieked and clamoured.

I don't think it was snowing
as she glided around the circumference,
lost her footing and nearly fell onto the fragile patch of ice
where beneath the surface weeds, like serpents, coiled.
I don't think it was snowing when all those nights she was led
behind the ice rink's bleachers by one boy or another flashed
before her and she saw in the sky's dangerous transformations
the double-edged possibilities for how her past errors
might be reflected if she did not change course.

I don't think it was snowing
when so lost in the thrust and *glide, glide, glide,* the noxious, delirious,
blinding rhythm, she reached the eighth circle. She skated faster,
past the apparition of the souls of the evil impersonators,
the souls of the counterfeiters, the souls
who bear false witness. She skated by all of those
who stood frozen and affixed by the transgressions
of the coldest wind until she reached the ninth circle
and her wonder was planted on the beautiful lone skater
in the middle, wearing a cloak dark as Satan.

I don't think it was snowing
as the skater began the triple axel, his cloak fanned out
like black wings, three distinct but silent faces
flashed at her in turn, and though she desired nothing more
than his deep gaze burning into the curves and valleys
of the forbidden, a sudden gust, like a gentle hand,

took her in its arms, lifted her from the centre of gravity,
and thrust her spinning (into the twilight) across the frozen lake.

THE ADOLESCENT SUICIDE

   I think
she knew the day she rode
the rapid transit downtown
to meet her great-aunt for lunch.
She must have walked,
jean jacket tied around her waist,
blond hair bleached
by the sun, past the local Chinese restaurant, a pub,
rubbing her free hand along the slab of a building,
ear turned to hear, the way a small boy puts his palm
to the tracks to feel the vibrations
of an oncoming train before crossing
to the other side.

   Metallic,
industrial sky, between concrete slabs
the crocuses push though.
Past the Terminal Tower, the arcade,
the Euclid mall, kicking through a mass
of city pigeons. Overhead
the buds held back
on the depressed,
twisted trees.

   The afternoon
the great-aunt took the girl to lunch,
her eyes were like a tree
without force, a sky without colour,
a story without a legend.
I can just imagine it,

the girl at the table,
sorrow-less, clear, and cognizant,
the choice having already been made.
For once, her mind un-
encumbered by complication,
deliberate, without appetite.
To please her great-aunt,
the beloved orders her last meal:
A turkey sandwich. Pickle on the side. Diet Coke.

THE FALL

Hollow, gargantuan gym, yellow wood floors polished slick
as a bowling lane where during the week boys in damp T-shirts

ran their laps, wrestled, kicked ass, on Saturday afternoons
was the private sanctuary where we slipped on our white gloves

and black leotards, fled the trapped air of our mothers'
station wagons for finishing school. Beneath the vapour

of ammonia the boys' gym still reeked of their sweat and hormones.
But as the autumn leaves held fast to the fertile maples and oaks

that regaled our suburban block, it was the girls who empirically
reigned. Self-possessed, confident, she turned on the phonograph,

diagonally moved across the room. she was nearly airborne.
Suck in your abdomen. Imagine a string holding your head high.

Sixteen girls fell into line. Was there any talk among us?
If so, no one remembers it. Only the exposed pipes on the ceiling,

the cling clang of the enormous furnace, as the descent began.
When we left the coterie of girls, and the padded, protected walls,

entered the thaw of those fall nights, led almost blindfolded
into the eerie cavern of the backseat of a boy's car,

there was no spring. No summer. No golden chariot.
Even the moon, changed forever, was abducted into darkness.

The wind, like a slap in one long swoop, stripped
the trees naked. Desire was indistinguishable from suffering,

from thought, from all that we had understood.
And yet, all those years in private under the cool quilts

of our beds, or in the cluttered attics of our minds, we craved it,
this terrible reckoning, where free of constraint, cleansed of regret,

we stepped out of ourselves, discarded our fears like clothing,
and entered the gate where love lived whole and breathing,

capable of both pain and beauty. It was all this we ever wanted
offered up like a shiny pomegranate: his breath on our neck,

his sex still governing the room, without our knowing it,
even when the last whistle had been long blown,

the last boy showered, locker slammed, lock turned,
long after the last boy had begun the endless walk home.

VIRGIN SNOW

It happened, not as we had hoped,
underneath the stars, or along the banks
of a lake, or in an empty pasture,
but shut in amidst a virgin
snowstorm. It was among the coats and castoffs
on the bed in one of our parents' bedrooms,
they having vacated the premises for some exotic island
just, we naively imagined, so we might have our tryst.
The sensation, if I had to describe it,
was like stepping over the edge
of a cliff into water and not quite knowing
how deep the fall or whether we'd surface again.
I wish I could say it was sublime,
but here is what I remember:
the smoke and liquor like a halo
over the room, the scratch
of his rough jeans on my thighs,
the parting, swift as an axe
splitting wood in half.
Downstairs the party in full
motion as if Bacchus himself
were hosting the celebration
fully aware,
as the ball dropped
to announce the beginning of the new year,
and sailed down the long tunnel of Eros,
of what temptation would lead to.
There were no bells,
no feelings of enlightenment.
Later when I was alone in my bed
I thought one thing: What if it was true,
that in the end *he* was irrelevant?
I waited all night but not once did I hear
the nightingale fill the sky with reason,
or glimpse the sun muscle through the sky
to announce the birth of the miraculous.

A DREAM OF WINTER

The sky weeps
like Persephone released

from the underworld
to favour us with flowers.

I am half awake
and if I close my eyes

I will be gone again.
Who are you

who are so close
in dream?

The ground with all this wetness
sinks beneath my feet,

so much desire
behind me

I must have dreamt away
an entire lifetime.

It is so hot we imagine
we'll never endure

such heat – these summer storms,
these brief flashes

of lightning, promise
a coolness long since bargained for.

Sleepless for want of you,
but if I take your hand

I disappear.

RAPING THE NEST

We found the blue small eggs inside the intricate nests
painstakingly made of twigs, hair, and down,

powerfully held them in the palms of our hands
like something fragile we might crush.

We were young, bored girls stealing eggs from a robin's nest.
I held one egg and shook it. There was a viable

tight little knot of life hot inside.
I wanted to crack it open to see what made it beat

so wildly in my hand. Above us in the sharp
summer air flocks swooped down making V's in the sky.

The days blended carelessly into one another
but, on this afternoon, because there was a boy I desired,

I did not care what would live or die or one day
fly into the air like the soul released from the body.

In the outline of the farthest branches I imagined his hand
on my face, the long complicated veins on his arms.

TEMPTATION

Day was nearly breaking when we awoke.
The winter storm was abating.
It was the first day of creation.
I did not care that we had no money.
That what was between us was still as fragile
as the sheer of our curtains.
We had returned from Italy.
The image of Christ's hand
raised in blessing, the face of the Virgin

suffused with light, the naked
Child was in my head.
I thought of the divine foreknowledge
that lies behind her strange smile
and I wanted it.
Last night's storm hit so hard
the tree had fallen, exposing
the writhing roots, the marks
like scratches where it had hit on its bark.
I ached for something greater
to take possession
like sap in the belly
of the tree
necessary
to go on living.
The entire city was snowbound.
Ice formed intricate crevices
along our window. The trees
along the tree-lawn
except for the one sacrificed
by the storm were bathed in robes of white.
In the harsh light of that evening
like the force of two celestial planets
colliding into one, I felt it take hold.
I pictured the fresco, the gold light
circling her head. The stab
so severe it sliced into the centre
of my being. When we peered
out the window the scene before us
was no less serene or benevolent
than the nativity: the shadow
of the tree's icy arms spread out
like an angel's in the snow, the lip of light
cresting, the quickening of day upon us.
Through the reflection of our breath on the cold glass
I saw your round Italian features
distilled in the clairvoyant image
of the child. The wind picked up,

leaving no evidence
of how it might enlighten
or harm.

SEVEN SEEDS

I have been inside the third-floor walk-up
for months, like a bird confined to her nest.
I watch the sun press against the window
and filter through the veins and arteries
on the leaves of the cherry tree
in the little garden, the honeysuckle fading,
the vines slowly perishing.
     By now
she will have sprouted
fine downy hair. Fingernails. Inhaled fluid
in the fetal lungs. I have witnessed
the slant of sky at every hour
of the day. Winter passed.
Then spring. Now the world
is so bright.
     For one small peek
I bargain my confinement.
As I begin the walk
down the two flights of stairs
I know what it must have been like,
to see the fruit held out,
to know that soon she would be brought
back to her mother's warm-bedded
meadow and released
from the underworld.
     Without foreknowledge
of her doom, she must have said to herself,
Just one seed,
and then tasted it,

and then another,
until she had consumed all seven,
the juice staining her lips crimson.
The light was bright that day.
It is shut now in my brain
like the star
made of seeds inside the flesh
of an apple when it is cut
open and exposed to the elements.
Yesterday my child ignorant
of a mother's grief
took those seeds
and planted them in the garden.

LANDSCAPE WITH CHILD

Here I am for once on the other side.
Let me tell you what it's like.
There is barely a ripple on the lake.
Rain, yes, but we crave it, the temperate sound of water
on glass, on the wooden beams of our roof
and the sound of trucks on the road beyond the farm
breaking the perfect silence.
Our child sleeps now mostly through the night,
and when he comes in our bed we don't mind.
The horses in the barn have all quieted,
allayed by having endured last evening's storm.
We wake to the riot of birds
and we have vowed that we will learn their names
and families. It won't do to say the red bird,
or the blue one.
It is the same with these trees:
white pine, spruce, hemlock.
Yesterday a deer and her fawn crept behind a stand of them,
the fawn nursed, and the deer watched ahead,

on the lookout for danger so they might not come to harm.
Still we live in fear, but it is this field
of black-eyed Susans and bleeding hearts,
not their beauty, but how well they live without us,
we have come to depend on.
The deer and her fawn did not linger.
They shot through the open field
to the brambles and brush on the other side.
Who knew what would become of them.
We have learned to spot chicory and a spray of lavender.

THE SWAN

No matter the hour
of night or day,
she's there – always
at one shaded bank
of the pond
or the other.
Always alone.
Once, it almost frightened me –
she was in the centre,
not a ripple on the lake,
not her mate,
nor another wading bird in sight –
so regal and pure, and unharmed,
so unafraid, it seemed,
of solitude,
so sure.
Imagine, desire gone,
no longer essential.
Not touch, perhaps one luxury –
memory – to sustain her.

A WORLD FOREGONE
THOUGH NOT YET ENDED

It is your small body on my white sheets
curled up beside me, pulling at my skin
as if you want to get back inside,
that keeps me up at night.
Yours is the face I awaken to.
I watch your body growing plump with milk
and know every new fold and mark.
At night I sit on the deck and watch
the stars unfold. There is little wind.
I have forgotten what it was like when the moths
pressed against the light. The vibrant colour
of ripened berries.
The moan of an animal.
When he comes to me, half-filled glass
in his hand, wanting
me to touch him, I hear
you stir in your crib. I know what your body feels like.
The soft skin of a flower, not bruised, not yet
in torment. The wet crease at the back of your neck. All night I listen
for your wordless sounds.

HISTORY OF LONGING

On a clear day from the deck
you can make out on the horizon
the lip of ocean
and in the foreground
a spray of wildflowers and the fence
leading to the field where horses graze.
But what I love most is the moisture
of the sea in the air, the salt you would taste
on a child's skin if you were to kiss it,
and from one of the bedrooms
if you happen to wake up in the early dawn

out of fear you remember from childhood
and thought long since gone –
before you understood that love
is immortal –
you would see the iron dawn
break against the window
and hear the rise and fall
of sleepers' breaths in the other rooms.
And when morning had fully crested,
the sound of church bells.
From the road if you were to come up in the dark
you'd make out only the light on the porch
and the smoke rising from the chimney
like a signal from survivors of a wreck
but they would be strong enough to guide you.
But what if just like that it was gone,
the sky bereft
and the children hungry?

ORACLE

There was a chill in the ocean air,

despite the momentary surge of sunlight through the dense clouds,

but they were by the sea –

the ominous swoon of black birds overhead beginning

their necessary migration

in that small division of time

when nothing more was expected than this: to be together by the sea.

Shouldn't the child run between his mother

and father without fear

and shouldn't she hold her husband's hand

and shouldn't he watch from a distance

as she chases their child on this barren

stretch of eroding beach and amidst the sound of gulls screeching,

stench of seaweed, whip and pull of the wind,

shouldn't they hear the sound of laughter

though already the shadow has been cast along the beach?

A CHILD BANISHES THE DARKNESS

The child presides over our lives like the
blinding presence of tall white pines. In the
low room she hovers; she is the dark un-
tamed place, like a thicket in a neglect-
ed wood where I fall to after each new
loss, the unforgotten dream buried like
a small toy under layers of frozen
un-raked leaves. She is the hidden secret
we don't talk about because there is noth-
ing left to say. So much snow on the roofs
of tall buildings, along the cobbled streets,
in the eaves, and on the narrow bridge and
in the quiet palm of the newborn trees.
Nothing left to fear. All the earth is calm.

IN SEARCH OF THE SUBLIME

How did she have the courage night after night to extend herself
high and blind as a suicide into the unknown to grasp an outstretched
    arm?

I fled the balcony where Uncle Joe, bedecked in his lodge brother's hat,
reserved seats for us each year (he died of Parkinson's) and circled
    down

the back stairs. Behind an open door they kissed like star-crossed
    lovers.
The strange heat of it, how it could move air, or sand, or dust.

She is in the centre of the ring, the beam of light's sole focus.
Against the ominous timbre of the drum, the net drops.

Sequined, hair wrapped high in a jewelled tiara, leg held in arabesque,
forsaking tranquillity, in pursuit of reinvention, she flings

from one swing to another like an exotic, bedazzled bird
in search of the sublime. In one free-floating, heart-stopping

moment she is pawned off, like an undesired object, from one hand
to another. Deaf to the gasp-held hush, into the odour of damp hay

and illusion's grandeur, she looks straight into the eyes of immortality.
One slip of her lover's resin-coated foot off the rope, one beat

out of time, could kill her. We will all die, whether underneath
a tent of stars, or locked in the car's exhaust, or in a hospital bed.

The weak sun collapsed through the cracks in the canvas exposed
her caked-on makeup and ripped stockings; bleached-out costume;

her smile's gesture of despair – why hadn't I noticed before? –
as she took her final bow.

THE AVIARY

Out of nowhere came the ravenous sound and I knew she had
    returned:
the pheasant escaped from the pheasant farm down the road:

wire, the cage of sun through the rafters, hay, dried corn, the smell
of dampness, the incubation of light. Patient hens perched

over their clutch of eggs, their eyes fierce, maternal;
heads bent as if in reverence to the fragility of the unborn.

Winter hardy, able to withstand bitter cold, plumage faded,
pecking her bill against our deck like a careless mother

no longer living in fear of dishonour, no longer ashamed,
abandoning her eggs to feast on scraps of our evening barbecue.

In the half-life of an interior room and the wilderness outdoors,
the papery-thin soul of one being and another, we hear her:

the sound of persistence against our wood echoing its desperate
acoustic, the leave-taking and the return. The horrible hatching.

THE BOY BEHELD HIS MOTHER'S PAST

The ivory wedding hat came tumbling down –
how long had it been stored away, untouched
like desire repressed and bound –
and fell to the floor with less than a hush.

How long had it been stored away, untouched?
The boy beheld his mother's past
as dusk descended with less than a hush.
Was it possible her marriage might not last?

96

The boy beheld his mother's past –
Who was she? Who else did she love?
Was it possible her marriage might not last?
Light abandoned the skylight above
and shadowed the rug where they once danced.

Was his life governed by fate or circumstance?
The curtains trembled without a sound.
On the rug where they once danced
the ivory wedding hat came tumbling down.

THE BARBECUE

On the plywood deck canopied by Connecticut trees
so tall and lush we felt dwarfed and insignificant,
the family gathered under green leaves.

There was barely a scratch of wind or breeze.
Someone lit the coals, poured the drinks
on the plywood deck canopied by Connecticut trees.

A boy hammered a swarm of bees.
One of us mourned her unborn child.
The family gathered under green leaves.

The humidity was like another child between
us we wanted to take inside and send to her room
above the plywood deck canopied by Connecticut trees.

The child who took a fall with bruised knees
would never find herself, the third we would lose to cancer.
The family gathered under green leaves
on the plywood deck canopied by Connecticut trees.

THANKSGIVING PRIMER

The day I put my son's life in danger
even the fragile vase on the coffee table

was wiped free of dust, sparkling like the lights
around a nativity pasture at night, for our newborn's

first Thanksgiving. In the pale of morning,
unaware of tragedy or consequence,

still marvelling that only six months ago
I had not known love to incarnate both

sorrow and happiness before I felt the grasp
of his small fingers, or the way the light

intensified when it cast its shadow in his room,
or the sound of a bird once I knew it would be the sound

he would hear, nor had I understood the necessity of milk,
the brilliance of knowledge, or ever prayed more

for the goodness of humanity, I turned my back
to my son teething on his plastic ring in the centre of my bed

to baste the turkey. In an instant I heard the fall
on the wood floor, his piercing cry

containing all the pain and chaos of the universe.
After our blessings, platters of cranberries, sweet potatoes,

roasted turkey passed, I was still shaken.
How many times would I harm or put myself

before my son – and how would I know –
and like a child wrongly solving an equation

on the blackboard – the frail sound of chalk, its fallen ash –
what would be my punishment?

THE ARBORIST'S LAMENT

Tiny and red and rows and rows of them
like the eyes of the gods or the garnet
of a necklace. How they shimmer, how they
replenish like pure, unadulterat-
ed love. If I were an arborist in-
fatuated with trees, I'd sit under
the cage-like lattice of bark in winter,
a full-leafed skirt in spring to study their
twisted nature, it would be these tangled
vines climbing the mesh I'd most desire. Prune
and prune, and still more rows until the mind
is beside itself, full to the brim, in-
toxicated. Inside such soft membranes.
What more is there I don't yet understand?

ATONEMENT

Along the bank
of the Hudson

in late September
the first day of the new year

we broke bread and threw it
into the river. Nine days later

from dusk to dusk
we do not eat. We thirst.

Early evening, a screen of light
behind the river. It is time

to forgive, to ask why
we still hold on.

Across the water
in that golden world

wildflowers fade,
shadow stains the grass,

the trees still regal
in their green armour

carry the weight
of a long history

of suffering
which in a month's time

will have let go.
We are weak from hunger

for love withheld
or unknown,

for what we've lost
and can never attain.

Even that small imperfect
flicker of light

is nearly extinguished.
High-pitched wail

of a lover's cry,
a deserted playground

in the distance.
Resolve crumbles

like the bricks and mortar
on our ancient temples.

Birds flock
and assail the sky

like a mass exodus.
The sun falls.

PUMPKIN PICKING

The day we take our son into the orange fields to go pumpkin picking,
he proudly wheels the wagon through the muddied rows

stopping now and then to observe the pumpkins,
how one is lopsided, another the shape of a woman's torso,

one the size of an October moon. Before us the grey, fractured sky
so close you feel you could walk into it and enter the other world,

the air the kind of cold you pray for by August.
By the side of the road a man is burning leaves, the smell drifts

through the tangled rows, seeps into our wool jackets, our hair,
the way loss penetrates every aspect of a landscape, from a frozen

patch of ground, to this stand of blue spruce in the distance.
While my son is strutting down one row, up another, filling his wagon,

kicking one pumpkin that has broken loose and begun to mold,
I wander farther into the field through so many rows of orange heads

it's as if the souls of our lost children have entered this graveyard
where in a month's time the fields will be picked over, pumpkins

splayed, smashed, left to rot. Ready to be pulped, seeds cleaned,
toasted, later carved into jack-o'-lanterns, these pumpkins haunt me.

How they grow wild, almost arbitrary, how they give so much
meaning to a boy. Look, their thick, husky umbilical stems

wedding them to the ground, how with a quick slice of a blade,
even a hearty pull, they are cast free from the earth toward heaven.

from
INTRUDER
(2008)

But what's art but an intense life – if it be real?
HENRY JAMES, *The Lesson of the Master*

DEMON LOVER

Is it still snowing?

Yes, she said.

Will it go on?

It will blanket the earth, she said.

It will fall

Over the hidden valleys and seep

Into the bark of the trees.

It won't end, she said.

Will you stay with me?

I won't leave, she said.

I must go then, said the lover.

THE SEDUCTION

It was ablaze, the room in the apartment building
facing the back courtyard where the poet slept,
and she woke not to the sound of sirens
but to glass breaking, voices shouting, Get out, get out,
and in her half dream she thought they were pranksters,
boys on the loose, wreaking havoc
in the courtyard between the two buildings.
Get dressed, he said, rushing into the room,
Just in case, and both thought about their boy
asleep in his bed, hoping they didn't have to wake him –
he was afraid of fire.

They walked to the picture window,
she in her long T-shirt, her husband already dressed
(prepared for disaster), and watched the fire –
it had spread into the courtyard between the buildings
determined to find all the unknown
private spaces and corridors.
There were small barrels of fire
like bonfires made to keep warm.
The engines drew close, the ladder
stretched out to the sixth floor
where the blaze bled flames strangely quixotic
and the hoses went off with such force
the water punctured windows, ricocheted off brick,
and it was gorgeous, dazzling,
the orange and reds of such ruin.
Once the water met the flames
the fire transfigured into smoke so thick
they could no longer see the fire trucks, the ladder,
the darkness, only grey, gaseous, colourless, ethereal
matter – still in half-dream –
she thought it must have been her internal desires
gone askew, reincarnated into the fist
of a god warning her against her window,
or Michelangelo's hand of heaven
seducing her toward what frightened and compelled her.
They watched in disbelief,
bewildered by how quickly
the destruction had started
and how it consumed them.

THE FIGURE

From a blank canvas sprang a swirl of colour and emotion:
a mysterious figure emerging from a dark thicket.

Was he beautiful? Did it matter?
For once ugliness could be a form of beauty: an equivalent

to prove the soul's existence.
Dried paint like a second skin on our hands, its oily smell –

was it possible to replicate love?
The paintbrush unleashed a river of blood.

The day darkened in the room. Time lost track.
We forgot our mothers still in bed, the failure of fathers,

secret lives of our sisters. Is it the figure's mystery
that enthrals or the shock of seeing manifest the passion

we longed to hide? Is he our stillborn twin or a lost love
buried under the debris of daily existence? Or the terror

of loss itself? Brutal hands, a slash of red.

THE POET CONTEMPLATES THE NATURE OF REALITY

On the side of the road a deer, frozen, frigid.
Go back to your life, the voice said.
What is my life? she wondered. For months she lost
herself in work – Freud said work is as important
as love to the soul – and at night she sat with a boy,
forcing him to practice his violin, helping him recite his notes.
Then the ice thawed and the deer came to life.
She saw her jump over the fence, she saw her in the twilight,
how free she looked. She saw her eyes shiny as marbles,

as much a part of this world as the fence a worker
pounds into the earth. At night she still sat with the boy.
He's learning "Au Claire de la Lune."
Do you know it? He has established a relationship
with his violin. He knows that it takes practice to master it:
the accuracy of each note, to wrestle his feelings to the listener.
But he's impatient. Sometimes what he hears and feels
are not always the same. *Again*, the poet says.
She knows if he tries to silence his fervour, he might not ever know
who he is. The poet contemplates whether a deer can dream.
Rich blood-red berries on a branch, pachysandra in the garden.
A soft warm bed in the leaves.

MUSIC IS TIME

Music is time, said the violin master.
You can't miss the stop or you'll miss the train.
One, two, three, four, one, two, three, four,
one, two, three, four.

She clapped her hands together
as the boy moved the bow across the strings.

One, two, three, four, one, two, three, four,
one, two, three, four, the violin master shouted,

louder and more shrill so that her voice
travelled through the house like a metronome,
guiding him, commanding him to translate the beat,
to trust his own internal rhythm.

Good boy, she said.
See how hard you have to be on yourself?
How will your violin know who you are
unless you make it speak?

RULES OF CONTACT

A ball is cracked into the air and the underlings
in their red caps field it. A line drive; another

to the boy at third. *Get under it. Don't be afraid.*
Let's hear some chatter. It's late in the day.

Have you noticed that everyone is separating?
a mother from the bleachers remarks, knitting

her anxiety into careful knots. *Where are the sparrows?*
The sun rests over the awning of trees,

wind's compass stopped, gone awry.
One boy refusing to comply steals second.

Is disorder a rally against resignation?
Boys bow their heads beneath the sun's glare.

The boats along the Hudson move in slow motion,
unmoored from the dock.

How to quell the current rising against the boat?
How to trust what moves beneath it?

The Lord of the Field hits a high fly,
in homage to his disciples. *Look alive.*

Get behind the ball. Stay on top of it.
Hurled faster than the speed of light

the ball travels from one boy's mitt
to another boy's in perfect orchestration.

My son won't let me kiss him any more,
a mother on the bleachers decries.

THE POET CONTEMPLATES HER CALLING

Come to me, he said, *I want to touch you.*
I will never disappear. The voice was deep and resonant
as if it belonged to her true nature. Some nights
enchanted by the voice and its lyric resonance –
the memories it evoked – she could hear nothing else
save its desperate music. *Stay with me,* he said, *don't go back,*
and the divide between the real and invented
grew like a split in a canyon.
She thought the tender dinners, open window
at the table to allow in fresh air,
their private chitchat sealed off
and protected as if underneath glass
inside the insular walls of their home might be enough.
That she could still follow what compelled
through the narrow courtyard down the unsafe, spiral stairs
and into the mysterious garden if she managed
to live with the disturbances, and she continued to travel further,
to seek more, forgetting she could never turn back,
even when the voice grew so faint she could barely hear it,
to ponder what she had left behind.

CATHEDRAL OF WONDER

They peered into the hole in the broken stained glass of the cathedral
and the boy saw that it was a sculptor's studio in the basement

of the grand church, all dust and plaster and half-finished
sculptures in abundance. *I don't feel like myself any more,* he said.

The boy was eight. He knew how to read, play music, calculate
his times table. He had abandoned one set of heroes for other heroes.

The biblical garden lush with autumn flower, the morning brash,
brilliant, curling itself inside and around the open spaces within

the close, the boy's eyes on fire as he glimpsed an interior world
viewed through a broken window. Through the peephole he watched

the sculptor chisel into the body of the statue; witnessed
the mysterious alignment of faith and vision turned out of stone.

Her face is in pain, he said, unaware of suffering in pursuit of beauty.

MYTH OF CREATION

With nothing but a pencil and a blank sheet
of thin-skinned paper the empire forged itself
without will or reason upon the dreamer,
luring her toward reciprocation until the tip
of her finger formed a callus, until word
by word, sentence by sentence, sense by sensibility
found their own scurrilous logic.
Trust me, said the voice, who seemed to be
a second self, a shadow. *There is no free will
without pain*. A touch against her skin
signified the fragility of being, the elusive trees
were her fathers, books her teachers; her heroes
were statues in the museum garden.
She travelled through the city, its history etched
in the brick of marble buildings;
searched faces for meaning though not one face
struck her alike. *Don't be afraid*,
the voice said, as if fear were another definition for happiness.
And for one moment the world revolved
around her like a sea of shimmering stars
where she was the centre of the universe,
where she shut the door and no one dared enter,
where she dreamt of lovers who would never want her,
where the rain fell regardless.

THE POET CONTEMPLATES THE INTENSITY OF EMOTIONS

Like extreme weather, volatility
has the ability to threaten the stability of any field.
The poet suggested that if she were not moved
when the kindergartners sang "My Country, 'Tis of Thee"
facing the American flag, if the woman on the subway
mumbling to herself did not provoke memories
of lost relatives in war, if snow on the cornices
of the library did not excite her, how could she be expected
to believe in the longevity of passion?
If she did not awaken some snow-swept mornings
restless, filled with a desire she could not name
or replenish, then how would she know
when she was happy? (Did the marriage counsellor
really suggest she hide her despair? Aren't secrets forbidden?)
The winter has been cold this year.
When the weather comes on the evening news
there's reason to stay up late. Wind chill. Snow drifts.
Arctic temperatures. Fog against the window.
What does God have in mind, giving us snow again,
when for so many winters we've been deprived?
Snow of our childhoods, snow of our dreams,
snow falling on the train from Moscow
to Saint Petersburg when Vronsky followed Anna,
convinced he could not live without her.

INTIMACIES: PORTRAIT OF AN ARTIST

1. THE SEEKER

Has she nothing else to do
lounging on the bed in midday
while the young artist
perches on a table at the footboard
staring at her naked body?

On the table is a bowl of fruit.
Through the slats in the blinds
light slashes shadows across
the woman's body like wounds.
Held in the sealed envelope
between her crossed legs,
a promise. Her face bears
the look of agony. His of wonder,
of pleasure. Or perhaps she is the seeker
looking inside the boy's eyes
just before he bares himself
so that she might rescue her dignity.
So that he might lose his.

2. ADJOINING ROOMS

She poses in a room
sombre as a still life.
The floor cast in the orange stain
of a pumpkin, the blood orange
of a fruit cut open like a burst
of brightness. No one penetrates.
No one escapes the black-blue walls.
Her hair is long and wavy as a girl's
but gone grey and coarse.
Her naked body lures us closer,
permits us to see too much.
In another room her daughter practices.
In satin bodice and tutu,
in white tights and silk toe shoes,
hair pulled back tightly in a bun.
Her hands reach out into pirouette.
The two faces are the same.
One the hue of the other.
A twin odour reigns.

113

3. SLUMBER PARTY

It is the navy blue light
of a suburban evening when all myths are born.
Through the open windows, through the light from the sky,
the leaves on the branches sparkle.
Twinkle like lights on a party boat.
Two boys inhabit the low alcoves of the hot attic.
Two separate selves existing in one boy's room.
Always one wants to be like the other,
wants to possess him.
(They're not brothers.) Oh, to be the boy
whose back is turned, wearing only his white briefs.
He kneels in front of the TV as if to a saviour.
The other boy is exposed, naked.
He enters the open white sheets,
the trundle underneath pulled out in invitation.
On top of the TV an erotic doll
spins, casting shadows in the room.
Will the boys always turn against each other?
Will the doll stop spinning? Will the shadows
of our boyhood selves cease to be?

4. SATURDAY NIGHT

Don't be afraid. Come closer.
It's bath time. The boy's in the tub,
Father's shaving, Mother is dressed
in her evening wear: black silk slip,
high heels, leaning on the tub's edge.
Listen as she inhales her cigarette.
Listen to the splash. It's intimate. Private.
Feel the humidity rise, hear the slide
of the razor shimmy down Father's neck.
Watch the little boy pee into the water.
Look into Mother's eyes. What truth
do they belie? Is she no longer enchanted?

I know you feel you've intruded
on their privacy, entered their secrets
and lies, invaded their private space.
I know you want to leave. But the boy,
he's you, isn't he? Doesn't he make you ache?

5. FAMILY VACATION

The Ping-Pong table is available.
Do you want to give it a try? To volley with me?
Or perhaps you'd rather watch the nudes.
Look how comfortable they seem sprawled
on their inflatable mattresses in the sand.
The little girl with her long pigtails,
she's old enough to be his daughter.
The middle-aged women in their string bikinis
walking the beach, the feckless teenage boys
sparring with their rackets, the woman reaching
for higher volume on the boom box,
the one-armed man, what casualty befalls him?
It's tropical here. Take my hand.
You're getting too much sun.
The dog of some uncertain pedigree
digs his paws into the sand.
It's uncomfortable this time of day.
No shade. No trees save those palms
in the distance. Watch out. Shield yourself.
He's ready to run.

IN CONTEMPLATION OF THE HUSBAND

Suitors lured her away
with promises of secrets and abandon.

She was a locked door
without a key, a house without windows

to peer in, or perhaps he neglected
to seek her out.

His razor and comb gather dust.
The coins in his drawer are tarnished.

Private disquisitions, mysterious glances,
blood and grief woven into the epic of cloth

too precious to unravel.
Sometimes in moonlight's disguise

she thinks she sees him peering into the garden.
Rich forest and burn of wind on his skin,

voiceless wonder of her dreams,
recanting the nature of their attraction.

In proof of her theorem he strings his bow
and shoots a piercing arrow.

By dawn it is all erased.

ANNIVERSARY

The bouquet was on the table.
It was a bouquet of fall flowers,
day-lilies and red chokeberries,
gold daisies and purple hibiscus,
too robust for the vase to contain.
She had consulted with the florist.
A desire to name each family,
not to forget. *Lady in Waiting*:
a strand, with a chain of little red flowers
and a thick husky stem.
All week the bouquet had dropped petals,
filling the table with debris,
yet still she replenished
the vase with fresh water,
not wanting to let it die.
It was a grand arrangement.
By week's end it began to stink
slightly, that smell of warm, rotting,
humid earth, of something
that had simmered too long,
that needed new air to breathe.
She tried to cut the stems
to preserve them longer.
They were too thick to sever.
She took out the withered stalks,
making room for the flowers that still held on.
Her floor was a mess
of broken stamens and pollen.
Her sink was all petals,
where they'd bled.
There was more life left. *Not yet.*
No.

INTRUDER

He was quiet.
He wasn't speaking.
He was quiet unto himself.
That's what she liked about him,
how he took her to lost places
and uncovered secrets inside her
she longed to disclose.
How his presence gave her the will to do so.
How his quiet hunkered inside him
like a baby curled in a woman's womb,
and when it was finally pushed out, there was a flood,
a torrential outpouring of mucus and blood
and then this live thing kicking, crying, screaming,
demanding she pay attention. And then once she did
he was gone again, curled up, fast asleep,
sucking his thumb.

She drove through the park and noticed
the leaves had almost changed completely.
Where had she been?
The trees were red, orange, yellow,
leaves falling everywhere when before
it had been green, tame, lush.
How close she was to missing it.
The sun pressed up against the passenger window.
She was the passenger.
She longed to stop time.
Hold the trees. Stop the leaves from turning.
Get her hands dirty.

The intruder turned his head toward hers.
He kissed her. He traced her face
with his hands.
He had no name, no shape,
no voice, no familiarity with anyone she knew.
She had to face the fact that he was in her dreams,
beckoning her to follow.

She had to face the fact
that the leaves were turning, fading,
before she could rejoice in their demise,
that it made her crazy
how red and brilliant they became
before they died, how she wanted them to keep
changing, or not.
How she wanted to stop.
How she didn't want to change
and not know who she was
and whether she even liked the intruder
dressed in his cloak of many colours.

THE END OF LOVE

She was in her kitchen,
with the cool blue impenetrable quiet
she had craved and she remembered
the excursion of his warm hand
on her skin, the idea of a family
he had embodied, the strength
of his love for her still intact,
like a city underneath the earth
that had failed to fully prosper.
She remembered the day they had met
when they were young and different,
and she probed that moment
as she did all things until she was exhausted
by the what-if and whatnots and what would come to pass.
She saw her entire life pass
into all the objects in the house,
and she was reminded
of the familiarity of a full life as she had lived it:
the symmetry of colour, of shapes so perfect
you didn't want to touch or disrupt

the arrangement; the orchestration of their bodies;
how they had grieved,
the quiet distillation of his essence,
filling her house with breaths
so unlike her own.
When it happened, it came as something inevitable,
without expectation, without notice,
with a life and force of its own,
changing everything, even the quality
of air they had grown to depend on,
and they hadn't known how to stop it,
and then she knew it wasn't the end,
it was only the beginning.

THE SKIERS

I

It begins with snow. The lone wilderness.
An intruder, high in the silver hill
top. A racer, he swiftly glides the slick
mountain back, slips between startled lovers –
no forewarning. He leaves a trail of Ss
in his track. Breathless, he lies in the snow
beside the frozen wonder of the lake,
stirred by the intimacy of lovers.
How long since he tasted the bittersweet
sap running through the maple's heart, or stopped
to listen to the language of the lark?
All the young squires in their down jackets
and stocking caps surround him. *Follow me,*
Pandemonium high on the crescent.

II

She thought it was a dream. She couldn't
breathe. The voice was in her head, inside the clat-
ter. It stole from her. She couldn't see. Snow
kicked up. A blizzard of emotion; in
its wake a blur of black – the terror of
happiness rushed past. He whispered that she
was beautiful. A lark. She looked ahead.
She tried not to listen. It was as if
in that glance she saw her entire life
pass: passions set awhirl in blinding am-
bition. Who would she be if she turned back?
The cold hurt. A branch fell. She followed the
loops of her betrothed's trustworthy path, a-
gainst fierce wind and gradient's resistance.

III

The racer scans the enormous valley.
It's all snow, a field, a paradise of
white. Lovers locked in an embrace against
an evergreen tall and grand, its branches
appear to yield seeds of awareness. Her
face like a jewel, too bright to steal. He stops
at the ledge above the Great Divide to
navigate his path, springs forward and sails
again between them. She loses footing,
tumbles. Is it a dream, that voice she hears
as he dangerously whisks past? The guard
calls out in warning. Clouds disperse behind
firs and tall cedars. A black-tailed magpie
cries. The racer is banished from the slant.

IV

The wind changes direction. Rushing through
steeples of evergreens, spruces, sighing,
moaning, causing fragile branches to creak,
turning ground asunder. Where is the new
snow? The slope is rock, patches of broken
ice, clumps of trodden grass. The imprint of
a body fallen from the cliff. Injured
wings braided in snowy patterns. How bit-
ter, wind. How cruel. Underneath an over-
pass a divide of water. Evergreens
crowned with tinsel. Beneath the frozen lake,
schools of hungry fish. Ashes shiver. Is
there any light left in the cold mountain's
interior? The wind does not subside.

V

Or is it simply the sun's shadow spread
over the valley toward the village to
tell the rest of mankind the intruder
is not alone? *Don't follow*, the shadow
seems to say. It is treacherous, the moun-
tain air, the elevation, dips and gaps.
Don't be tempted. The dark unreasoned path
and miles of vacant powder camouflage
the lack of undergrowth. Two bald eagles
mated for life unless one dies leave their
sturdy treetop nest made of scraps of twigs,
soft moss, feathers to scrounge for the remains
of the bodies of the weak and lost who
did not survive their desperate hunger.

VI

Suspended over the sunken valley
from the lower bowl to Earth, the racer
traverses into winter garden. Dead-
fall, unforeseen rocks and boulders. The wind
is forbidding. An avalanche set loose
in the path. All a blur. A mirage of
white. She cannot see beyond the madness
of evergreens where not even a hawk
has trespassed. He falls with her. And as they
fall is aroused to love her. In fury,
unsure of fate, as if they are still a-
lone, desperate to circumvent the past,
they bed in a froth of wet leaves against
the eerie echo. The terrain is marked.

VII

Who is to judge the argument? The sky's
fury. Where is the red-tailed hawk, the scrub
jays, magpies, ravens? Is there no spark left
in the mountain's core? Can no living thing
survive without passion? The skiers are
alone, naked and spent amidst the grand
peaks. She cannot breathe. The mountain air ex-
hausts her. Was it all a dream? Bright powder,
voice in the wind, swiftness of its power
to transfigure. Leaves fix to her cold skin.
The dark gem of the heart a conundrum.
Descending gracefully down the slope, comes
the banisher of the interior,
offering warm blankets of devotion.

VIII

There is a tear in the dark sky. No light.
The slopes are cold, barren. The lone racer
traverses the mystique of the Great High-
way called Chaos where only daredevils
have crossed. He has fallen off the slope, his
skis no longer seduce the bare mountain.
He is alone, besieged by the shadow
of the peaks. The sun has scourged the slope, un-
burying patches of scruff and mud, a lost
scarf, a necklace of tinsel. Dwarfed ever-
greens litter the path. Gone is the blind pu-
rity, the sparkle. The earth's exposed to
its fundamental state without the van-
ity of beauty to obscure its fate.

IX

The mountain is forever divided.
The back bowl and the forward. The quarrel
in the wind does not subside as if caught
in a vortex forever in mourning
for the unchangeable past and yearning
to break free of its stronghold. *Who am I?*
Night's owl calls. Snow accumulates. It can-
not stop. The earth tastes its sweetness. The side
of the mountain is spare, free of tree and
vegetation. Dark, unseasoned, as if
there's a breach in the mountain's heart. Where are
the hummingbirds, jays, and falcons? Once wild-
flowers dotted the bluff. Bald eagles soared
over aspen. Now mist obscures the view.

x

Across the peak the shadow of a deer
and her hart neither frivolous nor star-
struck and her slender, spotted, just-born fawn,
legs still twisted from the womb, tucked behind
and licked almost clean of its smell to pro-
tect from harm as if to remind of the
possibility of love. Once two bucks
in agony fought to claim her scent. Un-
furled by the ferocious wind, aroused, snow
blows in circles, exposing what it meant
to conceal. One version of paradise:
Artemis, goddess of fertility
and the hunt transformed into a stag. For
one moment the world is perfectly calm.

THE POET CONTEMPLATES THE SUNFLOWERS

This is how she imagines it. A stillness.
He enters the room and is not afraid.
Once the poet watched a fence being torn down
picket by picket. It was white and surrounded a garden.
Inside the garden was a bed of sunflowers.
The toughest flower. She cut their stems
to put in a tall vase on her table
and it was as if she were cutting through a cord.
The poet likes sunflowers in the garden
where they are a part of the earth.
It was a mistake to have taken them indoors.
The black centre face-to-face with her
at the table, stems almost as tall,
the crown of yellow petals.
It was a mistake to take something from the soil
in which it grows and try to separate it

from the kingdom of its parenthood.
They knew each other a long time ago.
They were twins in another life.
A psychic who lived in the back apartment
read her cards when she was young and afraid.
Nightly the poet watched the psychic's clients trail in
eager for news. *Will my daughter get married?*
Will the baby survive? Does he love me?
Who am I? What do you see?
The poet can see things he doesn't want her to see.
She knows what his body feels like and they have never touched.
She knows that when he says he can't see her
it is because she is all he sees.
She knows when he says *don't,* it means *please.*
She doesn't know why she has designated him as the keeper –
it's not rational – as if only he held the key
and once unlocked, what?

THE POET DISCOVERS THE SIGNIFICANCE
OF THE OLD MANUSCRIPTS

It was a book as complex and profound as an epic masterpiece.
A book filled with pathos and history. A book about writing
brushes and inkstones. A book of betrayal and lust and madness.
A book that wanted to devour its reader with desire.
"Its innards were once fiery hot," the book said.
It had survived hundreds of years. They were at the Morgan
looking at the lost manuscripts of erotic poems under glass.
The poet thought of all the colours of pain
and suffering, not to mention the joy it required
to make one single line of verse. Or fiction.
She sat on a bench afterward drinking cold bad coffee
and denouncing the chapter on passion. "Press down on the hairs.
Let the writing brush . . ." There was no sun. It was a grey morning
and her small feet were frozen in her open-toed sandals.

126

She would forgo the book of songs; she would forgo
the book of laughter; she would forgo the book of acquisitions.
She would forgo the book that held no other equivalent
in life save the rush of pure feeling dripping like ink
from a pen. She had read that according to Daoist
medical theory the body contains in microcosm
the essential force of the universe, or chi, which is made up
of the male principle, yang, and the female principle, yin.
Each wanted to imbibe the other's life force.
She was free to write her own discourse.
All those colours flooding her, moving inside her.
All those words. They were rushing from her pen.
Making strange loops on her paper.
They'd been drinking, it was a long night of drinking
that frightened her.
They'd made it up her stairs and into the small room
the size of a closet. He was so tall he had to slump a little
and when she looked up at him it was like looking up the lean walls
of a building. *Please,* she said. *I'm here,* he said.
It was hundreds of years ago.
It was during the days of poems written about sheaths,
days of unwrapping long beautiful robes. Days of prose poems
and lotus flowers. *That perfume. Did you put it on for me?*
And then in the daylight, out in the open, where they'd gathered
to conduct a business of lies and forgo the book of knowledge,
forgo the book with no name, forgo the book of nights
and reminiscences and the book of declarations,
he cut her with a knife.
She was bleeding a blood with no colour.
A blood no one could see or touch.
She looked up at the tall building
and it was made of stone. It was a new day.
The modern windows the colour of jade.

THE BEAUTY OF THE CLEARING

She wanted to run. She experienced
the desire in its opposite form, the beloved
fleeing, and when she witnessed
the impulse in herself she felt like one of the actors
trapped beneath the spotlight of a stage; caught, a fraud.
Once the lights went on, she didn't want to leave
her seat, still held captive inside the drama though by then
the cast had retreated to their private dressing rooms.
Without the stage lights, the furniture looked old and shabby,
the floor dust-ridden, an inner dimness projected
on the lifeless stage. The desire to run
was instinctive – it was like running through a forest
dense and crowded by tall poplars,
she could only go one way, following the path
into the open clearing where she sought succour and sensed relief.
The trees slender and indestructible, the earth soft
and pliable beneath her feet. Not a tremble.
She had gone to see the new production
in a mood of disengagement and while
she felt the director had miscast the morphine-
addicted mother she was drawn in nevertheless,
and during intermission, the theatre abuzz
with the play's tension, she was moved
to find that an audience could be persuaded,
that the play – Long Day's Journey into Night –
had not seemed dated. A man behind her whispered
that the "whole fricking family was co-dependent"
and at the drinking fountain a young woman
said in O'Neill's hands all relationships are dangerous.
There was one point in the play, Act 4, where she wanted
to jump from her seat and command poor Jamie, the sad, misbegotten
brother (the poet, for God's sake), to leave, flee.
She still waited, hopefully – as if she expected
the characters to change – for the burden to lift,
though she had seen the play before
and knew the inevitable ending.
The true story is this: the beloved
simply wanted to hold her.

The beauty of the clearing, other than the warmth of the sun,
was its steady ground and lack of agitation
(the birds preferred the denseness of the wood).
There were two kinds of light—
light that kissed the tops of the trees
and hence the branches bent
toward it, and light that was destructive,
that absorbed the leaves, taking
a piece of their pigment—and she had never known
how to distinguish the two; better to find
solace in the shade. But it was something else.
When she reached the clearing she lay down
on the grass. The sun was shining.
She discovered it was in the ring of sun
where she longed to be,
it was like being reborn. The ability to hear
and see and feel without fearing
she was depriving someone else
of happiness. And in the clearing she understood
this was happiness.

THE DREAM

She was walking away from the house,
down the winding road, farther into the field
past where the horses grazed, through the straight
rows of the grape orchard, beyond the peasant farm
until she could no longer see the roof, the deck, the fence.
Could no longer hear the shots from the hunter.
She felt no attachment to the sky and its incandescence,
no attraction to the shifting of the earth
and its unseasonable cracks, no affiliation
with the cardinals or the scavengers.
All of it was gone – all meaning

she had attached to the significance of life.
She looked at her hands and did not
know them. She touched her face
and felt nothing. Not even want.
She looked at her body and was unclothed;
no one could find or see her.
She walked without destination
or distinction no longer understanding
who she was or where she was going
or whether she had ever understood
the meaning of cherishment.
Time past and time present and time future
had distilled into the oblivion
she once understood as sky.
She kept walking unsure why
she had wanted to be free.

THE POET CONFRONTS THE SELF

She took off his coat of envy.
She took off his sweater of anger.
She took off his shirt of resentment.
She unclothed the beauty of his torso,
cast free his cloth of pride, unpeeled
his mask of vanity, unadorned his ambition.
She released the falseness from his heavy shoes,
the want that bored a hole in his flagrant heart.
She unbuttoned his pain.
They were in the woods,
having detoured from the path,
luxuriating in the sounds of forest life,
the various and variant calls of birds,
trenchant, deliberate, delighting
in their laughter.

Is this who I am? he said,
naked of the wounds
of his multifarious nature.

DREAMING OF TWO WORLDS COEXISTING IN HARMONY

Odysseus lived with Calypso on the island.
She did not want to let him go. He drank nectar and ambrosia,
slept in a cave next to a nymph who wanted to make him immortal,
but each day he sat on the same rock gazing out at the sea
weeping for home and Penelope. Back home Penelope waited.
She was like a lighthouse, reigning over the seas, calling him home.
Outside on the deck the poet read about ancient wars and vendettas,
about a son protecting his mother from the dangers of her suitors.
Inside the Knicks were on and she could hear the cheers
and cursing through the screen. On the lawn were two birds,
one pursuing the other, darting through the trees,
creating cacophony and havoc. The long stems of the cosmos
bent in the wind, and then a sound as primal as a first cry
called over the mist, the screen door slammed shut,
and across the field she saw the little one sneak away next door
to fight another war on Nintendo.

AN ESSAY IN TWO VOICES

I

Imagination transfigures the image of the loved one.
The process of falling in love, Stendhal wants to persuade us,
is a process of crystallization. Perhaps you fancy lying in an orchard
looking up at the sky through the branches, how pleasant it would be
to be there with your new acquaintance. She is someone
who would share your feelings for the orchard and the sky.

But suppose now, as is highly probable, you meet
with "some coolness or slight rebuff " on the part of the person
with whom you are falling in love. Whatever the original hopes,
doubt gains a place in your feelings. Perhaps the other
is indifferent; perhaps the initial hopes were misplaced.
Perhaps under the transforming powers
of imagination, there's evidence of a positive attitude toward you.
This is what Stendhal thinks of as the "second crystallization";
and it is at this stage, he believes, that love becomes fixed.

II

The lovers are kissing under the glare of traffic lights.
They have walked for hours along the promenade near the park
in serious deliberation. They have been having the same conversation
for a year now. But we are in a relationship, she says. I know, he says.
What will happen when you leave, she says. *I'll go back to my life.*
What am I? she asks. *You're not my life,* he says.

TOUCH-ME-NOTS

She brought a little of the country into the city
in the pots of impatiens she had planted.
The petals white, pure, the opposite of colour.

She had transferred the impatiens from the garden,
digging her hands into soil two parts fibrous loam,
one part leaf mold and peat moss and pushing
the roots into the earth. Despite the quality
of the soil – its rich decomposition of life –
still they would not last. The plants were hardy
and tender, with thick stems and dark green leaves,
the seed-pods inside waiting to release, the air
awash in pollen. She looked into the flower
as into a pair of beckoning eyes offering
sustenance independent of a body, free floating
and regenerative and wholly belonging
to what was impossible ever to touch.

SNOW IN APRIL

It was snowing when I remembered faith –

I always prayed for it when it seemed that prayer was all I could do.

The snow was fine. It misted over the stark trees and formed a layer

over the things I care for, the shapes of buildings, the windows,

the little bushes along the library. The snow reminds me

there is another world I have forgotten because I always forget

how much I love the snow until the air begins to smell of it,

until the sky impregnates and then succumbs.

I had lunch with a friend who reminded me of my sister.

She died in April – the cruelest month (just last week we were touched by a warm spell and the crocuses had the audacity to show themselves).

I saw in my friend the torment one sees in those who have the need

to understand, to discover, to know, to transcend

the landlocked self. She was beautiful, with her black hair

(though my sister's hair was blonde) and the little wrinkles

that formed between her eyebrows when she was thinking hard.

And all along I thought we had to be together to be in love.

I thought we had to share the same roof,

the same child, the same bed.

THE SURFERS

Look how beautiful they are in the distance
Sliding on their boards as they embark
Into the white swirl and cascade
Back and forward. They always take
One step back before they move ahead
On the wave's long journey.

Follow me. Get on your board. Journey
To the breakers in the distance.
I know you're afraid to embark,
To ride the dangerous wave and cascade.
The crest of the breaking pocket takes
the body into the swell ahead.

You're thirsty. All of us are. Ahead
The beach is still. Seagulls mock the journey.
Once we took a fall and lost our way in the distance.
The ocean pulled us under and we embarked
Into the lure of the known and cascaded
Beyond our depth. The sea is not afraid to take

The restless. Or those who forget to take
Caution. The swell is deceptive, look ahead.
Face what threatens to destroy the journey.
Remember one surfer's funeral in the distance
Of memory's long shore? We embarked
On a procession to honour one boy who cascaded

To his death. He rode the cascade
From boy to man in one day. The waves take
Regardless. Is it worth losing what lies ahead?
But if the surfer refuses the journey
How can the wave close the distance?
There's no way back except to embark

Forward. What use is there to embark
Upon the crest of the unknown cascade
If not to enter a new precipice? Take
My hand. No one knows what lies ahead.
Or how to steer the journey.
I know you're tired. I sense the distance

Between us, the vast cascade, the resistance
To embark. The distance ahead.
Take heart. There's meaning in the journey.

THE DREAM LIFE OF THE POET

Everything passes, said her friend, and she waited for it to lift
like fog on the winter beach, bringing clarity – .
She could barely make out the seagulls pecking the sand for crabs,
though she heard their horrible squalls, nor could she see
beyond the turbulence, past the crashing waves into the calmness
of the water. She had always longed for the sea, the way one yearns
for a different life, the dream life
not filled with down-to-earth demands
(she forgot to pick up the dry cleaning),
so that when the actor appeared, reckless, without responsibility,
stepping off one stage into another, she was inside this quandary,
and imagined a life they might have together.
It was a game she played with herself, knowing that he was an actor,
and the world of the stage took precedence.
I want it all, he had said, in a way that seemed seductive.
They were sitting on a bench, lunch hour in the park,
and he confessed he had never allowed himself really to fall.
She took it in the way she took in all things sensual.
It was April, the air still frigid, but she felt the warmth
in the breeze at her cheek and she leaned
toward it, moving her body so that she faced the sun.
In dreams begin responsibilities. She was afraid
to say it aloud, to break the spell. It had been a long winter.
She had attended a show at the Whitney
and was repulsed and provoked by the inflated, comical breasts
John Currin painted on his women, and the strange, twisted, bearded
men – caricatures, she thought, though as the show progressed,
the two naked fishermen at sea,
its nod to Winslow Homer, and "The Lobster" still life,
she understood Currin's grotesque figures were a reaction,
that everything is a reaction to something else.
She stared at the actor. He was good to look at, and in another life
she might have wanted to look longer. *Why do you like to act?*
He stopped picking the paint off the bench with his nail and checking
the coded message on his cell phone. *Because I'm not me.*
The sun fled to the other side of the park
leaving the bench desolate. It was too cold to be outside
and she had never been much of an actress.

NOTES

from *The End of Desire*

p. 9 The epigraph is from 'Thirteen Ways of Looking at a Blackbird' by Wallace Stevens. Acknowledgemnt is made to Alfred A. Knopf Inc., New York and Faber and Faber Ltd, London, for permission to reprint an excerpt from 'Thirteen Ways of Looking at a Blackbird' from *The Collected Poems of Wallace Stevens*, copyright 1923, copyright renewed 1951 by Wallace Stevens.
p. 31 'Without': this poem is a response to the painting 'The Dream' by Pablo Picasso, 1932.
p. 32 'Ironing': this is also a response to the painting 'A Woman Ironing' by Pablo Picasso, 1901.

from *Subterranean*

p. 145 The epigraph is from Ovid's *Metamorphoses*, Book V, translated by Mary M. Innes.
p. 82 'The Fate of Persephone – IV: The Fruit': some of the descriptive imagery in this poem are found passages from an article that appeared in the *New York Times* Magazine.
p. 103 'A World Foregone Through Not yet Ended': the title comes from a line in Hart Crane's 'Postscript'.

from *Intruder*

p. 129 'Intimacies: Portrait of an Artist' This poem is inspired by the following paintings by Eric Fischl: 'Bad Boy', 1981; 'Bayonne', 1985; 'Saturday Night' ('The Aftermath Bath'), 1980 and 'Saigon Minnesota', 1985.
p. 151 'An Essay in Two Voices': This is a response to Stendhal's 'Love' and his interpretation of falling in love as a process he terms 'crystallization'. The first section of this poem is an attempt to paraphrase a small part of his argument.
p. 144 'The Poet Discovers the Significance of the old Manuscripts' The following fragments of this poem are taken from two poems in *Chinese Erotic Poems*, translated and edited by Tony Barnstone and Chou Ping (Everyman's Library Pocket Poets): "Its innards were once fiery hot." from 'A Poem about a Broken Copper Flat-Iron' and "Press down on the hairs. / Let the writing brush…"

137

from 'A Poem About Writing Brushes and Inkstones'.

p. 148 'The Dream': The line "Time past and time present and time future' is derived from T. S. Eliot's lines "Time present and time past / Are both pehaps present in time future" from 'Burnt Norton' in *Four Quartets*.

BIOGRAPHICAL NOTE

JILL BIALOSKY was born in Cleveland, Ohio. She studied at Ohio University and received an M.A. in Writing Seminars at Johns Hopkins University, and an M.F.A. from the University of Iowa.

She is the author of the poetry collections *The End of Desire, Subterranean*, a finalist for the James Laughlin Award from the Academy of American Poets, and *Intruder*, a finalist for the 2009 Paterson Poetry Prize. Her poems and essays have appeared in journals such as *Paris Review, American Poetry Review, Kenyon Review* and *The Atlantic Monthly*. She is author of the novels *House Under Snow* and *The Life Room* and co-edited, with Helen Schulman, the anthology *Wanting a Child*.

Jill Bialosky is an editor at W. W. Norton & Company and lives in New York City.

Also available in the Arc
INTERNATIONAL POETS series

LOUIS ARMAND (Australia)
Inexorable Weather

DAVID BAKER (USA)
Treatise on Touch

ALISON CROGGON (Australia)
The Common Flesh

SARAH DAY (Australia)
New & Selected Poems

KEKI DARUWALLA (India)
The Glass-Blower: Selected Poems

GAIL DENDY (South Africa)
Painting the Bamboo Tree

ROBERT GRAY (Australia)
Lineations

MICHAEL S. HARPER (USA)
Selected Poems

SASKIA HAMILTON (USA)
Canal

ALAMGIR HASHMI (Pakistan)
The Ramazan Libation

DENNIS HASKELL (Australia)
Samuel Johnson in Marrickville

DINAH HAWKEN (New Zealand)
Small Stories of Devotion

BRIAN HENRY (USA)
Astronaut
Graft

RICHARD HOWARD (USA)
Trappings

T. R. HUMMER (USA)
Bluegrass Wasteland

ANDREW JOHNSTON (New Zealand)
The Open Window
Sol

JOHN KINSELLA (Australia)
Comus: A Masque
America (A Poem)
Lightning Tree
The Silo: A Pastoral Symphony
The Undertow: New & Selected Poems
Landbridge: An Anthology of
Contemporary Australian Poetry
ED. JOHN KINSELLA

PATRICK LANE (Canada)
Syllable of Stone

ANTHONY LAWRENCE (Australia)
Strategies for Confronting Fear

THOMAS LUX (USA)
The Street of Clocks

J.D.McCLATCHY (USA)
Division of Spoils

TRACY RYAN (Australia)
Hothouse

MARY JO SALTER (USA)
A Kiss in Space

ELIZABETH SMITHER (New Zealand)
A Question of Gravity

C. K. STEAD (New Zealand)
Straw into Gold
The Right Thing
Dog

ANDREW TAYLOR (Australia)
The Stone Threshold

JOHN TRANTER (Australia)
The Floor of Heaven